TROPICAL FARMING ECONOMICS

TROPICAL AGRICULTURAL SERIES

The Tropical Agricultural Series, of which this volume forms part, is published under the editorship of D. Rhind, C.M.G., O.B.E., B.Sc., F.L.S., F.I.Biol.

TROPICAL FARMING ECONOMICS

MARGARET R. HASWELL
B.Litt., M.A.(Oxon).

Additional Fellow, St Hugh's College, Oxford
University Lecturer in Agricultural Economics

LONGMAN

LONGMAN GROUP LIMITED
London

Associated companies, branches and representatives
throughout the world

© Longman Group Limited 1973

First published 1973

ISBN 0582 46670 9

Set in 10/11 Times New Roman
and printed in Great Britain
by
J. W. Arrowsmith Ltd., Bristol

To my fellow workers in the field –
to my many friends on the
farms and in the villages
and to D.S.G.

Preface

It has been fashionable development tactics for dealing with the subsistence sector of the low income countries of the tropics to assume that the farmers will automatically accept plans for agriculture because they seek to maximise output. To this end, development economists have collaborated with the technologists in programming for diversification and intensification of agricultural production to call forth the substantial surplus which is urgently needed to feed an increasing number of non-agricultural workers. But the cultivator who is dependent primarily on family labour has remained largely unwilling to exchange time-honoured methods for new productivity raising methods which demand greater human effort.

This widening gap between goals and achievement presupposes that advances in knowledge of the means of production have not been counterbalanced by a proper understanding of the motives for production. In this text, an attempt is made by reference to actual practice to shed light on farmers' responses at a time in history when rural areas of the tropics must be prepared for yet higher populations in absolute numbers in the decades immediately ahead, even though they may expect the share of agriculture in the labour force to decline.

Although the practices examined make no pretence to being a comprehensive cover, the evidence they afford does provide a new dimension within which to re-think policies, and translate them into action, for firmer assurances to small-scale farmers that the business of farming can be made an attractive proposition; and that it pays to stay in the village.

I am indebted to the Overseas Development Administration of the Foreign and Commonwealth Office, London, for permission to draw from material I obtained in Mindanao in Southern Philippines during two periods of field research in 1970 and 1971, for which I received financial support under their research scheme R.2227. I am also indebted to Mrs E. Lukes for her work in producing the typescript.

11 August 1972   M.R.H.

Contents

Plates

ACKNOWLEDGEMENT

TROPICAL FARMING ECONOMICS in our Tropical Agricultural
Series **by HASWELL**

We are grateful to Annual Reviews Inc. for permission to use Table
IV, from the article entitled 'Economic Bases for Protection Against
Plant Diseases' by Ordish and Dufour which appeared in the *Annual
Review of Phytopathology*, Volume 7, 1969.

List of Tables

Introduction

The central problem for low income countries is that the number of young people eligible to enter the labour force is growing more rapidly than the number of jobs available for them to fill.

What hard core of urbanisation can support an agricultural region which is overwhelmingly large?

In correlating urbanisation with industrialisation, has the 'modern' world failed to recognise what is perhaps one of the most critical phenomena of the age, that of the mushroom growth of towns which feeds upon a subsistence agriculture sector which it enslaves in a perpetual cycle of borrowing?

This begs the question whether we should not enquire into the apparent static position in granting municipal status to townships which might have reached a population density which demands this recognition, and the infrastructural benefits which it bestows.

Dependable measurements are needed to ascertain whether the growing small towns are more often situated near the periphery of already existing cities, thereby adding to the phenomenon of urban concentration, or are in the midst of the rural environment, thereby contributing to its more differentiated structure.

Few can be said to be attracted into agriculture; yet rural population percentages are overwhelmingly large in almost every country of the tropics.

Estimates based on a moderate increase in the total labour force of 1 per cent per year, with a 3 per cent rate of non-farm employment, under conditions in which agriculture's share of the total labour force is initially 80 per cent, indicates a decline in the absolute numbers in the agricultural labour force in the twenty-ninth year.

But the labour force in the tropics is growing faster than this, and is expected to grow appreciably faster in the future. However, growth of output rates cannot be accelerated simply by transferring labour from agriculture to industry and manufacture.

There is an old adage among peasant communities of the tropics that it takes 'six hands of farming' to make the transition from slash-and-burn shifting cultivation to the point where there are clear economic advantages of farm as compared to city employment; and that it is a slow process of change.

There are a number of reasons why it is unrealistic to review the record of agricultural production growth in isolation from all other factors.

Though water for irrigation is a high priority in narrowing the time factor in the development process, roads are of even greater importance.

In so far as inducement to acceleration of agricultural development is proposed by encouraging a substantial inflow of peoples from densely to sparsely populated areas, without a proper understanding of land rights and social and economic structures of the 'traditional' environment, conflicts and 'political' disturbances are likely to arise which could prove too high a price to pay in initial stages.

In terms of producer price, the immigrant who opens up an area of mature second-growth forest is no more favourably placed after two decades of 'taming' that forest, than is the trainee from an agricultural institute returning to his forest homeland who attempts to modernise in an area isolated by low population densities which permit the practice of slash-and-burn cultivation to go on unchecked. Both situations represent what might more precisely be called a point of discontinuity.

The producer operating in areas of sparse populations and new settlements can neither look behind him for the security he requires, nor ahead for the links which connect him with sizeable market towns and offer him an incentive to increase agricultural production. Transportation facilities are often inadequate; the cost of 'off-line' transport by porterage is virtually prohibitive; primary dependence even on the bullock cart imposes crippling spatial limitations.

But low producer prices are not always simply a function of high 'off-line' transport costs incurred by primary buyers who provide trucks where road conditions are poor; traditional practices, poor yields, and low prices, form a vicious circle which compels many peasant producers to borrow for food. In these circumstances, primary buyers in a given locality may not only be the main buyers, but also the isolated entrants to a market who have a vested interest in making such loans and collecting the kind payment at the time of harvest.

Much confusion arises from the prevailing tendency to project for countries as a whole a set of conditions which are a phenomenon belonging strictly to congested urban peripheries. What area of land does a man 'require' to produce his subsistence, and what would he like to have if he is to earn an economic living? It is the preoccupation with producing what is 'required' for subsistence of farm family households relying on hand-hoe or ox cultivation that constitutes the main area of unpredictability.

Two hectares per adult male engaged in agriculture is an assessment of farmers' decisions as to the amount of land they would like to cultivate; because this level of activity occupies such a large proportion of the population of the tropical world engaged in low productivity agriculture, there is a call for rigorous critical analysis of this area of darkness in which the real problem is not hunger but poverty.

'In the tropics, the theoretical environmental possibilities for plant growth often cannot be fully exploited because a perfect "fit" of cropping plan to climate cannot be obtained for natural or economic reasons.' (Duckham and Masefield, 1970.)

But explicit recognition and study of the problem involved in the provision of stocks against climatic uncertainty neglects the more deepseated problem of failures to improve standards of human health, with consequent deleterious effects on the efficiency of agricultural production. Failure on this front is in part a function of the isolation of rural areas from the services apparatus.

This leads us to examine one of the primary problems of rural 'isolation', the seasonal risk rut and, where rainfall is badly distributed, pressure of population on the water supply; the emergence of trading centres generating debt – the concentration in few hands of just those economic facilities as a shop, a small market, a central store, and a rice mill – to which peasant producers, whose energy has been sapped and whose agriculture has become inefficient through exposure to acute and chronic diseases, are prey in times of personal stress.

Labour in the busy periods has opportunities of being much more productive than labour at other seasons; and it is not only 'scarcity of season' that is overriding but, coupled with this, the 'health status' of farm family operators – their ability to maintain sustained effort, the effect of chronic sickness on managerial capacity, the willingness to innovate and to take risks. Even for the man who has escaped chronic or acute sickness, conditions at tropical temperatures are very different from those in temperate regions typical, for example, of the climate in the Scottish highlands where crofters in the early nineteenth century apparently reverted voluntarily to the arduous task of hand digging as a cheaper form of cultivation than the use of ox ploughs.

Can it be said, however, that low productivity activity in agriculture is a result of inertia?

Given well-tried methods over the generations, the local farmer may be expected to exhibit a shrewd idea of which of those modern methods that are presented to him it pays him to adopt. Such is the 'insecurity' all about him that a small economic gain may not be worth the having.

The conflict which arises among hand-hoe and ox-plough cultivators is summed up in the statement: 'As far as labour is concerned, it would appear realistic to expect male adults to work not much more than five hours a working day, and a total of 1,200 hours or about 230 days a year' (Norman, 1968).

And for that vast multitude of the tropical world which subsists by an economy in which cultivation is either entirely by hand or assisted by animal labour, there seems to be support for the theory that 'there is a rational tendency in developing countries for abundant labour being substituted for scarce capital in producing tertiary products thus inflating time devoted to such activities' (Bauer and Yamey, 1961).

It does appear from a number of economic studies, however, that there is a failure to take account of the component: status, prestige, and power, as a primary factor in economic development; and that while it may take the form of high leisure preference in a traditional agriculture setting in which labour is available for hiring from within existing social institutions, younger men may look for money wages in non-traditional occupations not so much as a means of acquiring the necessities of life (which are largely satisfied within the subsistence economy to which they have free access and which provides them with a sense of security), but for the consumption goods of a prestigious nature in the modern context of more affluent societies, which can be bought with money wages.

This concept of money sought for conspicuous personal consumption, while a low labour input subsistence agriculture is starved of agricultural investment finance for increased production from agriculture, is a phenomenon which calls for an examination of patterns of consumption as a prerequisite to an understanding of production processes. What are the incentive effects that consumption privileges (income) have on those individuals who seek employment in the non-farm modern sector?

'As the level of income or total consumption expenditures continues to rise, the expenditure on an item with an increasing elasticity of consumption tends to rise at a rate much faster than the rate of income growth' (Rosauro, 1961). This suggests that the luxury items which are identified by high elasticities of consumption tend to be the monopoly of the higher-income group of households. But actual practice among low-income small-scale producers does not necessarily correspond in any precise way to theoretical concepts. Even the poorest member whose total receipts may be well below the 'requirement' for subsistence may indulge in expenditure on consumption luxuries by resorting to borrowing from local money-lenders.

What are these luxury consumption expenditures? Education is found to be one of the most important criteria for prestige ranking; but to treat medical care as a luxury item concentrated among rural households of higher income levels overlooks an element of necessity in consumption expenditures when a working member of the farm family falls sick at a critical time in the agricultural cycle. Among the poorest households demands for production loans appear to exhibit certain characteristics: in one form or another they tend to be utilised for aids to human effort – the lightening of physical work, to replace a work animal which has fallen sick or died, to acquire sufficient 'power' to deal with those operations where timeliness imposes a severe constraint – rather than for biological or chemical inputs which will increase yields. But in poor rural communities where food is cheap in terms of prices of industrial goods, there appears to be little incentive to use industrial inputs in agriculture.

'The available evidence on the response of individual crops, of marketed surplus, and of input use suggests that though terms of trade may not, in themselves, be sufficient to bring about an agricultural revolution, they may accelerate or retard the growth rate initiated by a technological change' (Lele, 1971).

The retail or final price paid by the ultimate consumer is a measure of the welfare of farmers as consumers. Indications are that primary wholesalers' gross margins are not greater than transport costs, but that these become prohibitive for the transportation of low value products over long distances. The 'hidden' gains, or speculative profits, belong to the village trader who sells back to the producer at off-seasonal peaks at prices which correspond to those paid by the ultimate consumer in the city. When farmers themselves are both producer and ultimate consumer of their own product at prices paid by city dwellers, the producers' share of final price is transferred to the village trader, less storage and, in the case of foodgrains, 'mill later' costs. Although primary wholesalers' gross margins may therefore roughly be equated with transport costs, it is the extent to which producers make use of local buyers which indicates the degree of indebtedness for subsistence needs, and this in turn is a reflection of low output per unit of area. The high elasticity of demand for the consumer goods available in local stores frequently leads to enslavement in a perpetual round of debt which eventually becomes a cost to society in terms of production foregone through persistent poverty, and consequential inefficiency and ill-health.

'There are two sides to agricultural marketing. One side includes those activities connected with the movement, handling, storage, processing and distribution of food commodities from the time they leave the farm until they reach the final consumer. The other involves the movement of agricultural inputs from the manufacturer to the farmer' (Fletcher *et al*, 1970).

Leading inputs which contribute most to output increase are irrigation and fertilizer; but in many countries irrigation means simply the making up for insufficient rainfall by a simple device without adequate facilities of storing, field-channelling and drainage. 'It is when irrigation makes possible the introduction of a second crop, and when it makes possible increased application of fertilizer, the use of improved seeds, and farming techniques, that the quality of existing irrigation facilities must often be improved' (Ishikawa,

1967). The real issue to be faced is that the adoption of some cultural practices is associated with a level of irrigation which simply makes up for insufficient rainfall.

The mere application of industrial inputs by producers in these circumstances has not led to a shift in crop cultivation from one input-output combination to another with a higher productivity.

The role of additional labour input is not usually considered as a leading input. Yet we can hypothesise that total employment, and the structure of the farm labour force, including the factors which determine the magnitude of the working days for non-agricultural production, directly influences farmers' behaviour at all levels of agricultural production activity in early stages of economic development; and that it takes precedence over prospects for substantial increases in land productivity by an increased application of industrial inputs.

Of particular importance are the participation or activity rates, which can vary widely dependent primarily on the age structure of the population, the degree of female participation, and production foregone in terms of those members of the population in educational institutions who would otherwise constitute additions to the labour force. There is every indication that even the poorest families place a high value on education, and this is reflected in the heavy burden of debt which such households undertake. The private costs incurred in obtaining education cannot be seen solely as earnings foregone by the individual during education, but as net income foregone by farm family households through reduction of the family labour force, and the consequential increase in the dependency ratio.

In these circumstances, education becomes a consumption expenditure rather than an investment. For higher education is many times more costly than elementary education, and is invariably followed by the non-return to the rural sector of the school leaver or college graduate who all too often merely goes to swell the ranks of the city unemployed; meanwhile there continues to be a serious underinvestment in both the quality and the extent of elementary schooling and technical training in rural areas.

It has to be recognised that the problems with which the farmer grapples by reason of his consumption choices, which tend to dictate his production decisions and lead to misallocation of resources, are far more complex than might be inferred from a conventional analysis of resource constraints and technical change. In the ultimate analysis, the real problem with which subsistence-tied producers are faced is that they 'permit' consumption to outstrip production under conditions in which production is starved of investment finance which even when available, they frequently channel elsewhere.

Part 1
Rural 'Settlers' in Urban Settings

CHAPTER 1

The Growth of Rural and Small-town Populations

The ability of the ejido *to keep its people rather than letting large numbers of rootless proletarians drift into the cities where they are not needed, may still for a long time prove to be one of the really important benefits from Mexico's land reform*

Folke Dovring (1970)

It is not only that many of those countries which fall within that region which may broadly be termed tropical are low income countries; the central problem for these nations is that the number of young people eligible to enter the labour force is growing more rapidly than the number of jobs available for them to fill. This, as Dovring says even of Mexico – one of the more affluent – leaves all these nations a long way from the day when the agricultural population may begin to decline in absolute numbers; at least a generation and perhaps considerably longer.

This is the perspective within which the role of agriculture in the national economic growth of low income countries of the tropics must be viewed; with the dedication of the forester who plants for a future generation. In this sense development cannot be hurried; yet the urgency with which solutions must be found to alleviate the massive ills of multimillion modern cities – those isolated islands in huge deserts of rural poverty – cannot be ignored. In this context, time is on the side of no nation in whatever climatic zone it may happen to fall, unless the poorer nations can keep their people actively disinterested in drifting into multimillion cities 'where they are not needed'.

But the growth of agricultural production is nonetheless dependent on urban links. Hypothetically, the existence of a central city may be taken as the main criterion in the sale of agricultural produce because, by definition, investment in infrastructure will be large and transport networks highly developed. Under African conditions, however, of relatively low population densities and large tracts of semi-arid land, urban agglomerations of over 100,000 are still exceptional and, unlike parts of Asia and Latin America, this continent does not yet appear

4 Tropical Farming Economics

to be faced with the problems of overcrowding associated with multi-million cities. This does not preclude the existence of 'unmanageable densities' outstripping employment openings, and the provision of essential services in housing, public health, communications, electricity, and education.

What hard core of urbanisation can support an agricultural region which is overwhelmingly large? Philippine statistics, for example, define urban agglomerations as an administrative centre of cities and municipalities with a density of not less than 500 persons per sq km, or with a population of 20,000 persons or more. At the other extreme the UN Regional Center for Demographic Training and Research (CELADE) defines as 'urban' any population living in a place with more than 2,000 inhabitants.

In the recent past, there has been much preoccupation with the over one million cities, and those about to enter the one million mark – the unprecedented ruralisation of urban city squatters with haphazard, intermittent occupations, and no skills. How much less productive are these peoples when they leave the village than when they stay in the village? How great a dislocation do they cause in city transportation services, housing, sanitation, and health services? Human environment in the low income countries is not, as the western world believes, a matter of resolving problems arising out of development, but of

1. Rising expectations: young West African rural dwellers.

2. Can the land provide a living? A Filipino family trying their luck in
Mindanao.

tackling problems arising out of growing poverty and unemployment.

In correlating urbanisation with industrialisation, the western world
has furthermore failed to recognise what is perhaps one of the most
critical phenomena of the age, that of the mushroom growth of
towns which, far from supplying an industrial base generating
employment, are no more than trading centres generating debt. The
hard core of these towns feeds on a subsistence agriculture sector
which it enslaves in a perpetual cycle of borrowing to fill a 'hungry'
season gap between harvest and harvest. To this must be added
another dimension, the condition of health of villagers, which can be
fairly correlated with condition of road; compared with the urban
area, the state of health of village communities, with its consequent

3. The unprecedented ruralisation of urban city squatters.

effects on productivity, is at its very worst beyond points in which
feeder roads are so bad that villages cannot be reached in all seasons
at distances greater than 5 km from a paved highway. Many millions
of people whose energies are so urgently needed to produce marketable surpluses are trapped in just such a situation, and live in varying
degrees of helplessness dependent on the extent of periods of flood and
drought and other vagaries of soil and climate.

Simply to define as urban any population living in a place with
more than 2,000 inhabitants, without enquiring into the structure of
these 'small towns', being content to narrow the focus of attention to
capital cities and those which have municipal status, exposes the
agriculture subsistence sector to levels of insecurity and uncertainty
which have their roots in factors which are far more complex than is
generally admitted or understood.

4. Can the poorer nations of the tropics keep their rural peoples actively disinterested in drifting into the multimillion cities where they are not needed?

Wrigley (1971) reminds us that within the tropics, that area which lies between $23\frac{1}{2}°$N and $23\frac{1}{2}°$S of the equator, is contained about 40 per cent of the earth's surface; furthermore, three-quarters of this area is covered with water, and receives over half of the world's total rainfall. He states that

at the equator the period in the year when the sun is overhead is divided and the days during which it is overhead are shorter than at the tropics ($23\frac{1}{2}°$N and S). These three factors combine to make regions at the tropics where the sun turns, hotter in summer than at the equator. Outside other influences, the rainy season of the tropical region is associated with the passage of the sun overhead, which gives rise to a double rainy season at the equator and a single one at the tropics. The length and severity of

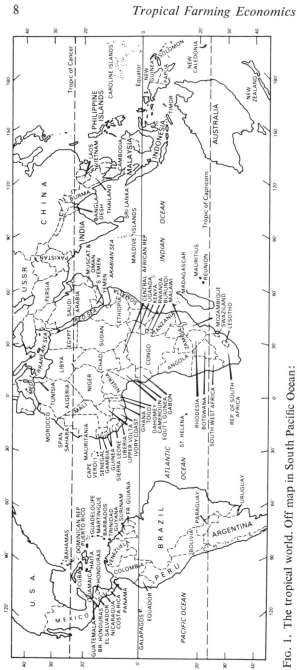

FIG. 1. The tropical world. Off map in South Pacific Ocean:

	Lat.	Long.
	° ′	° ′
Hawaii	21.19 N	157.50 W
Gilbert Islands	1.20 S	176.25 E
Ellice Islands	8.00 S	178.30 E
Western Samoa	13.48 S	171.45 W
Fiji	18.08 S	178.25 E
Tonga	21.09 S	175.14 W

the period between the rainy seasons determines the boundary between the rain forest and deciduous forest, and the suitability for certain tree crops such as coffee and plantains.

But the accepted climatic classifications are not much used by agriculturalists, Duckham and Masefield (1970) point out, for 'every farmer or local district seems, to those who farm it, to have a climate of its own'. However, they recognise only two classes of tropical agroclimatic regions, the 'wet' tropics and the 'seasonally dry' tropics. The wet tropics, they point out, are concentrated 'in a zone within a few degrees of the equator, and the seasonally dry areas occupy the outer latitudes of the tropics'. They stress, however, that there are important exceptions; for example, that the equator passes through a very dry area in Somalia and Kenya, while in south-east Asia wet conditions extend northward to Thailand and Burma and even beyond the tropic to Assam. Wet conditions must not, however, be confused with Wrigley's statement that a double rainy season occurs at the equator. Thailand, for example, is affected by the monsoons – referred to by Wrigley (1971) as 'the creation of high pressure areas over land masses in winter and low pressure areas in the heat of summer', which are of vital importance to the rainfall of India and south-east Asia. Thailand's rainy season extends from May to November; moist winds from the Indian Ocean to the south-west and to the south blow landward, and almost daily rainfall leads to annual floods over part of the country by September or October. While causing floods in much of the country, however, in one region, the north-east, rainfall is insufficient and local famines and food shortages occur in areas isolated by poor or non-existent roads during this season. Notably throughout the region the proportion of rural to urban population in 1970 was found to be extremely high by the Manpower Planning Division of the National Economic Development Board.

Data on the population of municipalities was collected in December of that year for the whole kingdom; Table 1.1 indicates the bias which would be created in confining major studies on economic problems to the central region in this example of high concentration of urban population in the capital city and its satellite towns, which are situated in this region.

This begs the question whether we should not enquire into the apparent static position in granting municipal status to 'townships' which might have reached a population density which demands this recognition and the infrastructural benefits which it bestows? Can we argue from the base of an area of land to which a population is encouraged to migrate from areas of high density and low agricultural productivity, to settle and begin clearing undeveloped sites? It is broadly stated in the Philippines, for example, that such settlements

Tropical Farming Economics

TABLE 1.1   *Urbanisation levels by region: 1965 and 1970 according to the registration data for Thailand*

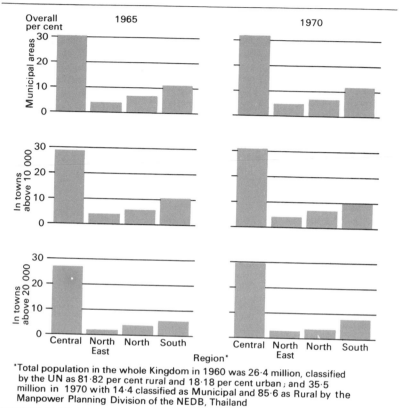

*Total population in the whole Kingdom in 1960 was 26·4 million, classified by the UN as 81·82 per cent rural and 18·18 per cent urban; and 35·5 million in 1970 with 14·4 classified as Municipal and 85·6 as Rural by the Manpower Planning Division of the NEDB, Thailand

take fifteen years to establish, eighteen years to reach a population and infrastructure suitable for a municipality (500 persons per sq km or 20,000 inhabitants), and thirty years to develop into an urban city with a population of 50,000 and over.

What is the evidence that migrants have resettled, or townships developed, in areas which in the very recent past have ensured a cheap source of food, in contrast to those cities of earlier centuries which tended to be sited on waterways as a cheap source of transport? Fig. 1 clearly shows the continuing prevalence of seaports among the very big cities of the tropical countries of the world; may there not be some correlation between the development of these cities from their original status as trading posts, and the present trend in the development of 'small towns' centred on trading in the 'cheap' food which is the major source of livelihood in tropical countries with more than

50 per cent of their total population engaged in low productivity agriculture or subsistence wage labour?

The neglect of 'small town' population is recognised in the UN (1969) estimates of the growth of the world's urban and rural population, from 1920 to 2000. For example, estimations of 'urban' population based on nationally defined criteria are liberal in Latin America – 'localities of 2,500 or more inhabitants in Mexico, administrative centres of districts and *municipios* having 1,500 or more inhabitants in Colombia, localities of 1,000 or more inhabitants in Venezuela (of which those having 1,000 to 9,999 inhabitants are classified as intermediate between urban and rural), and so on. The UN population study observes that

> because of the liberal definitions of urban population in Latin America, the rural population, as defined, increased appreciably less there than in South Asia and Africa where small towns apparently play a lesser role; the estimated rural and small-town populations in these three areas nevertheless grew more nearly with the same speeds. . . . Generally speaking, the figures suggest that small towns have been growing considerably faster than the more strictly rural population, yet probably slower than the localities of at least 20,000 inhabitants.

The importance of development problems in rural and agricultural areas renders it imperative that dependable measurements are made to ascertain 'whether the apparently growing small towns are more often situated near the periphery of already existing cities, thereby adding to the phenomenon of urban concentration, or in the midst of the rural environment, thereby contributing to its more differentiated structure'.

Established as a Registered Company in 1936 with Rs 600,000 capital, by 1961 the assets of the Rayagada Sugar Factory in Orissa State (India) had reached over Rs 10 million. Relatively inaccessible in 1936, land was obtainable for only Rs 125 per hectare and factory operators were able to obtain leaseholds for a nominal rent of Rs 12 per hectare; after twenty-five years of operation the value of land had risen fortyfold. In 1936 the proprietors of the factory pioneering in the area found a closed economy based on slash and burn shifting cultivation of low yielding crops of millet. The forest was so dense and tiger infested that it was unsafe to go out of Rayagada after 4 p.m. At that date, the population was 4,000 inhabitants; by 1961 the population of this small town had increased to 15,000 – a rate of growth per cent per annum of 5.4 (Haswell, 1967). This is a high rate of growth indicating a considerable net migration over natural increase especially when one takes account of the low growth rate for India as a whole in the decade 1930 to 1940 of 1·4 per cent per annum (Clark 1967).

TABLE 1.2   *Urban and rural population estimates for major world areas, 1950 and 1960*

	*More developed regions**	*less developed regions†*
Land area:		
Millions of sq km	61·3	73·8
Inhabitants per sq km		
1950	14	23
1960	16	27
Of whom urban per sq km		
1950	7	4
1960	10	5
rural per sq km		
1950	7	19
1960	6	22
Per cent of World's land area		
urban		
1950	62·1	37·9
1960	58·8	41·2
rural		
1950	23·3	76·7
1960	19·9	80·1
Population in millions		
urban		
1950	438	267
1960	583	409
rural		
1950	420	1,391
1960	394	1,605
total		
1950	858	1,658
1960	977	2,014
Urban population per cent		
1950	51	16
1960	60	20

* Europe, Northern America, Soviet Union, Japan, Temperate South America, Australia and New Zealand.
† East Asia without Japan, South Asia, Latin America without Temperate South America, Africa and Oceania without Australia and New Zealand.
Source: Growth of the World's Urban and Rural Population 1920-2000, Department of Economic and Social Affairs Population Studies no. 44, New York, UN, 1969.

From past records, the UN estimates indicate that 'it is reasonable to expect fluctuations in the growth of urban and rural population'; rural and small-town population gained only by one-tenth between 1920 and 1960 in the more developed major areas of Europe, northern

America, the Soviet Union, and Oceania, 'and it may gain only slightly in the four decades of the future'. The rural and small-town population of the economically less developed major areas of East Asia, South Asia, Latin America and Africa, however, increased by one half from 1920 to 1960, and in these areas UN estimates forecast that it may almost double from 1960 to the year 2000. It should, however, be borne in mind that the UN (1969) projections have been calculated before the results of the 1970 censuses became known.

CHAPTER 2

The Market for Labour

Few can be said to be attracted into agriculture.
The poor are held to the land by family and
cultural ties, by lack of resources which would enable
them to leave, by bonded servitude, by almost any
reason except a belief that there are economic
advantages of farm as compared to city employment

Arthur L. Domike and Victor E. Tokman (1971)

Johnston (1971, p. 37) points to historical experience as suggesting that 'change in the occupational structure of a developing country is a slow process, and the rapid growth of population of working age that now prevails makes it more difficult to accelerate the process'. Much misguided policy making and planning has arisen out of the deference paid by administrators to the builders of economic models based on data relating to the early developing countries, set as they were in a climate of external factors many of which have little or no bearing on the growth path of the late developing countries.

Johnston (1971, p. 9) postulates a situation in which the total labour force is increasing at a moderate rate of 1 per cent per year, and non-farm employment at the rate of 3 per cent per year; this would suffice to achieve a structural transformation turning point in only twenty-nine years (or a generation) if agriculture's share of the total labour force is initially 80 per cent. This is the point at which the absolute size of the farm labour force begins to decline. But, he points out, if the farm labour force is growing at 3 per cent with the same initial conditions, 'even a 4·5 per cent rate of growth of non-farm employment would only suffice to reduce agriculture's share in the labour force to 60 per cent in fifty years and the farm population of working age would still be increasing at an annual rate of nearly 2 per cent' (1966, p. 310).

In Table 2.1 agricultural population comprises more than persons actively engaged in agriculture; it also includes their non-working dependents. Nevertheless, it clearly illustrates the overwhelmingly large rural sector of almost every country of tropical Africa with as many as twenty-two recorded as being in the 80 per cent and above bracket. This situation differs radically from that found in Asia

TABLE 2.1 *Agricultural population as percentage of total population in the major tropical countries of the world.*

Country	Population density per sq km		Capital city	Population of capital city† ('000's)
			AFRICA	
Chad	95	3	Fort Lamy*	99 (1964)
Tanzania	95	14	Dar-es-Salaam	273 (1967)
Niger	91	3	Niamey	79 (1968)
Uganda	91	40	Kampala*	123 (1959)
Mali	90	4	Bamako*	182 (1968)
Ethiopia	89	20	Addis Ababa	644 (1967)
Mauritania	89	1	Nouakchott	15 (1965)
Sierra Leone	89	35	Freetown	171 (1969)
Somalia	89	4	Mogadiscio	173 (1967)
Gambia	88	32	Bathurst*	48 (1967)
Upper Volta	86	19	Ouagadougou	78 (1966)
Guinea, Rep. of	85	16	Conakry*	197 (1967)
Angola	84	4	Luanda*	225 (1960)
Cameroun	84	12	Yaounde	101 (1965)
Dahomey	84	23	Porto Novo	75 (1965)
Gabon	84	2	Libreville*	57 (1967)
Kenya	84	18	Nairobi*	478 (1969)
Madagascar	83	11	Tananarive*	333 (1968)
Ivory Coast	81	13	Abidjan*	282 (1964)
Zambia	81	6	Lusaka*	238 (1969)
Liberia	80	10	Monrovia	81 (1962)
Malawi	80	37	Zomba	20 (1966)
Nigeria	79	69	Lagos	842 (1969)
Togo	79	32	Lome*	135 (1968)
Sudan	77	6	Khartoum	194 (1968)
Rhodesia	75	13	Salisbury*	380 (1968)
Senegal	75	19	Dakar*	581 (1969)
Zaïre Congo	70	7	Kinshasa	902 (1967)
Mozambique	69	9	Lourenço Marques*	179 (1960)
Congo (Brazzaville)	65	3	Brazzaville*	136 (1962)
Ghana	60	36	Accra*	758 (1968)
South West Africa	55	1	Windhoek*	36 (1960)
			ASIA	
Yemen	89	26	Sana	60 (1956)
Vietnam, S.	85	103	Saigon	1,682 (1968)
Laos	81	12	Vientiane*	162 (1966)
Vietnam, N.	80	134	Hanoi*	644 (1960)
Thailand	78	68	Bangkok*	1,608 (1963)
Cambodia (Kmer Republic)	75	37	Phnom-Penh	394 (1962)
Saudi Arabia	72	3	Riyadh	225 (1965)
India	70	164	Delhi* (including New Delhi)	2,874 (1967)
Indonesia	67	78	Djakarta	2,907 (1961)

TABLE 2.1—*continued*

Country		Population density per sq km	Capital city	Population of capital city† ('000's)	
		ASIA			
Burma	62	40	Rangoon	822	(1957)
Philippines	58	124	Manila*	2,044	(1968)
Malaysia	55	32	Kuala Lumpur	316	(1957)
Ceylon (Sri Lanka)	50	187	Colombo	551	(1967)
Formosa (Taiwan)	47	384	Tapei*	1,605	(1969)
Singapore	9	3,471	Singapore*	1,988	(1968)
		AMERICA, CENTRAL			
Haiti	80	172	Port-au-Prince	240	(1960)
Guatemala	64	46	Guatemala City	577	(1964)
Honduras	62	22	Tegucigalpa	253	(1969)
Dominican Republic	59	86	Santo Domingo	655	(1969)
Nicaragua	58	15	Managua*	262	(1965)
El Salvador	57	158	San Salvador	341	(1968)
Mexico	52	25	Mexico City	3,484	(1969)
Costa Rica	50	33	San Jose*	349	(1966)
Jamaica	49	179	Kingston*	377	(1960)
British Honduras	45	5	Belize*	48	(1966)
Panama	43	19	Panama	389	(1969)
Cuba	35	72	Havana*	1,566	(1966)
Puerto Rico	25	310	San Juan*	754	(1966)
Barbados	24	591	Bridgetown	11	(1960)
Trinidad & Tobago	20	203	Port of Spain	94	(1960)
		TROPICAL SOUTH AMERICA			
Bolivia	63	4	La Paz	525	(1969)
Ecuador	57	21	Quito	496	(1969)
Brazil	55	11	Rio de Janeiro*	4,207	(1968)
Colombia	50	18	Bogota*	2,294	(1969)
Paraguay	50	6	Asuncion*	412	(1968)
Peru	50	10	Lima*	2,416	(1969)
Guyana	35	3	Georgetown*	103	(1969)
Venezuela	29	11	Caracas*	2,064	(1969)
Surinam	27	2	Paramaribe*	182	(1964)

* Cities marked with an asterisk are urban agglomerations;
† the years to which the figures relate are given in parentheses.

SOURCES: *FAO Production Year Book, 1967.*
UN Demographic Year Book, 1969.

generally in that population densities in tropical Africa are relatively low. Excluding the two extremes, Saudi Arabia and Singapore, and taking account of the size of India relative to other countries in the region, under Asian conditions population densities may be expected to exert a very different influence.

Of particular significance in tropical Africa is that, although it has not as yet been overtaken by the multimillion capital cities characteristic of both Asia and Latin America with their attendant evils of urban sprawl and shanty towns which are a direct consequence of heavy migration from the agricultural sector, a high proportion (especially in West Africa) have developed from early coastal trading posts dependent on a hinterland which, by and large, still remains in early stages of agriculture, employing little labour and virtually no capital. We cannot rule out this factor as a possible main contributor in the present relatively small size of urban cities in Africa.

Youngson (1967) stresses the importance of natural resources in economic development, and we have to recognise the basic positive natural disadvantages of many soils of tropical Africa in which rainfall is uncertain – low rainfall, excessive rainfall, and absolute scarcity of rain. Under conditions found in much of this continent of relatively low population densities and large tracts of semi-arid land, there is a close correlation between the percentage share of the total production of millets and sorghums, which are traditional foodgrains capable of withstanding severe droughts, and populations of particular countries whose production is directed mainly towards supplying subsistence consumption needs. In this context, Johnston's calculation that a structural transformation turning point can only be achieved in twenty-nine years (or a generation), or longer, has meaning.

Among those few African countries with a higher concentration of their population in urban areas, however, Ghana offers an acute example of a problem of urban unemployment which already exists and which is typical of many countries in both Asia and Latin America, in which there is a preponderance of young workers in the unemployed group with 21·9 per cent of the total open unemployed of 11·6 per cent in the age group 15–24 years (Turnham, OECD, 1970). Indications are, therefore, that although in some respects tropical Africa may be said to be more favourably placed than other tropical regions in the time span she can allow herself for development, failure of labour absorption is a threat which some parts of the continent can ill afford under present political stresses and current emphasis on rising expectations.

The African case generally of relatively low population densities and, by definition, less immediate problems of severe pressure of working population on the urban labour market, is in no way comparable to the Latin American case if one looks, for example, at the evidence for Colombia. A pilot mission under the World Employment Programme appointed by the International Labour Office (ILO, 1970) to appraise the employment problem concluded that 'Colombia's great asset, spare land, must be exploited, and that the agricultural sector will have to provide some of the five million jobs that are needed'. The Organisation for Economic and Cultural Development (OECD) quote an urban rate of unemployment in Bogota of all persons of 15 years and over of 13·6 per cent, of which 23·1 per cent fall in the age group 15–24 years. The ILO mission calculated that the rural population of working age is 'probably growing by 3·5 per cent a year or slightly faster' – more than twice as fast as agricultural employment has been growing in the recent past 'about 1·4 per cent per year'.

'If agricultural employment were to grow at this pace', the mission's report continues, 'jobs would have to be found in this sector for about 1·5 million more people in the next 15 years.' Such an expansion as 3·5 per cent in agricultural employment, or 100,000 jobs per year, apart from the financial resources required, would present organisational problems, including the opening up of transport facilities and the provision of credit and technical advice to a substantial fraction of the families involved, which would be extremely difficult to solve. For the sake of illustration, the ILO mission therefore take one-half:

> 1·8 per cent per year which would involve a moderate acceleration compared with the past. This would contribute about three-quarters of a million jobs towards the 5 million needed over the next fifteen years. To absorb the remainder of over 4 million would require an average growth of employment in other sectors of 7 per cent a year, and a growth of output of about 10 to 11 per cent per year.

Given these assumptions and the initial conditions of agriculture's share of the total labour force quoted by the mission of 50·5 per cent, the downturn of the agricultural labour force would occur in the eleventh year.

Turnham (1970) points out, however, that 'since the population groups from whom the 1980 labour force will be drawn are already born, projection of the active population is a matter of estimating future death rates applicable to the relevant population groups and applying the estimated participation rates to the survivors'. His results are shown in Table 2.2 for the countries of the tropics, and point to the important fact that the labour force in these regions is projected to grow appreciably faster in the future than in the past.

At the regional level, the Central American case is especially high with an alarming overall increase of the order of 50 to 60 per cent per

TABLE 2.2 *Estimates of growth of the labour force in the countries of the tropics: 1950–80*

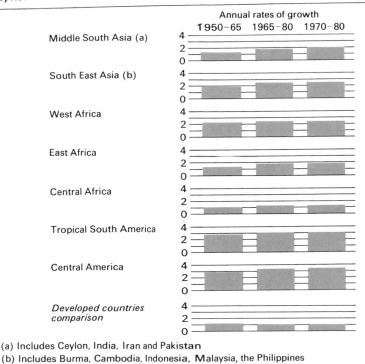

	Annual rates of growth		
	1950–65	1965–80	1970–80
Middle South Asia (a)			
South East Asia (b)			
West Africa			
East Africa			
Central Africa			
Tropical South America			
Central America			
Developed countries comparison			

(a) Includes Ceylon, India, Iran and Pakistan
(b) Includes Burma, Cambodia, Indonesia, Malaysia, the Philippines and Thailand

Source: David Turnham, *The Employment Problem in Less Developed Countries: A review of evidence*, OECD. June, 1970, p. 34.
(derived from data given in Ypsilantis)

decade. In arriving at these estimates, however, Turnham states that 'in the projections much the most important source of growth in labour force arises from projection of population changes and the overall influence of projected changes in participation rates is very small'.

Nevertheless, it begs the question as to whether Johnston is not overoptimistic in his calculation of a moderate increase in the total labour force of 1 per cent per year. While declaring his awareness of the rapid growth of the population of working age that now prevails, he still points to the historical experience of the United States, Japan, and Taiwan; in the United States it took as long as 138 years for the percentage of agriculture in the total labour force to decline from 71 to 5 in 1968, in Japan 88 years for the percentage of agriculture in the total labour force to decline from 76 to 19 in 1968, and in

Taiwan 68 years to decline from 71 to 49 in 1968 (Johnston, 1971, p. 37). Yet in so far as his projections refer to the African scene, his time scale may not be far wrong for much of Central and East Africa; but the problem appears to be facing West Africa more seriously already – indeed to an alarming extent, with an implied overall increase of the order of 25 per cent per decade or almost 40 per cent over the fifteen year period from 1965.

The slow growth rate of the urban labour market is indicated from analysis of available data in the Philippines (Haswell, 1970); for the period 1961 to 1966 the estimated annual average rate of growth of non-agricultural employment was only 0·874 per cent. But in a low income economy in which the majority of workers are in agriculture and there is a surplus of urban as well as rural labour, growth of output rates cannot be accelerated simply by transferring labour from agriculture to industry and manufacturing. Unless the productivity of the agriculture sector is raised at the same time so that a larger number of non-agricultural workers can be fed, their transfer will not be possible.

This is further emphasised by Rhind (1969) who draws attention to the fact that

> economic planners for development and betterment of living standards have not always understood the position in countries with a predominantly agrarian economy. . . . Without a rise in the purchasing power of the population, industry cannot flourish and with the bulk of the population in agriculture it requires a rise in agricultural incomes to support industry.

Rhind cites the classic example of Japan, where smallholdings and a large farm labour force have not changed over a century but where farm productivity has greatly increased; and he gives figures of average farm size recorded by FAO of about 1·0 ha in 1878 and 0·8 ha in 1962.

> Yields of rice rose from 1·8 mt/ha to 4·0 mt/ha in the same period. A significant thing about Japanese farming is that, while there has been a large rise in productivity, there has been little change over a century in farm size or labour employed in farming. There was, however, a large expansion of the non-agricultural sector which was thus able to absorb excess rural population. . . . A very important early change in the fiscal structure was from a rice tax paid by farmers in kind – a tax on productivity – to a land tax paid by land-owners in cash and used for promotion of industrialisation. . . . Japan's agriculture has retained the smallholder pattern characteristic of the rest of Asia. Both agriculture and industrialisation developed together but initially the resources for industrialisation came from agriculture (not from foreign loans) and the rural sector provided the main market for early industrial products.

There is an old adage among peasant communities of the tropics that it takes 'six hands of farming' to make the transition from slash-and-burn methods of shifting cultivation – the most primitive form of agriculture – to the point where there are clear economic advantages of farm as compared to city employment; that is to say, where modernised practices are followed, including the use of mechanical equipment and hired labour, and farmers are producing entirely for the market. This is a saying which deserves closer examination both for its time effects and for its area effects, and the support of empirical evidence for its acceptance.

Part 2
Farming for Survival

CHAPTER 3

Theoretical Progression through 'Six Hands of Farming'

Population growth is not necessarily adverse to economic growth

T. R. C. Curtin (1969)

Curtin challenges the prevailing view among modern economists that 'in the particular case of the developing countries their relatively high rates of population increase add to the considerable difficulties they already face in attempting to modernise their economies and achieve rapidly growing incomes'. Ester Boserup (1965) agrees:

> It is not to be denied that the food potential of the world has been narrowed down by populations who did not know how to match their growing numbers by more intensive land use without spoiling the land for a time or for ever. But neo-Malthusian theory is misleading because it neglects the evidence we have of those growing populations which have managed to change their methods of production in such a way as to preserve and improve the fertility of their land.

Historically, the fundamental advance in technology was the transition from food collection to food production because every other use which we have learned to make of the material universe has depended upon our ability to produce food for a given population by means which do not of themselves entirely exhaust the energy and time of that population.

There are, however, a number of reasons why it is unrealistic to review the record of agricultural production growth given in Table 3.1 in isolation of all other factors; the tendency to do so has all too often led to a highly dangerous practice of making such platitudinous statements as 'credible performance', 'rapid growth of agricultural production in comparison with the developed countries whose agricultural production rose no faster'. Technological advance alone places the late developing countries in a very different category from the early developing countries.

Meanwhile, Table 3.2 indicates that in several countries of the tropics agricultural production is rising less rapidly than population – most notably in tropical south America; and, more seriously because of the higher population densities in Asia, those countries in which growth in agricultural production appears to be hardly keeping pace with population growth and where the agricultural population in the rural sector is especially high – India is a classical example with a total population quoted by Mrs Indira Ghandi when she visited Britain in her capacity as India's Premier in 1971, of 550 million. Venezuela, on the other hand, a country with an overall population density of only about 27 persons per sq km, appears to have expanded agricultural production at a high rate despite her favoured position in possessing large oil resources; but the proportion of her population in agriculture is relatively low, which suggests that those who do farm make it their business because they see clear economic advantages in following this occupation rather than any other.

A remarkable count of trees, stumps, and anthills, was made in the late 1960s by Taiwanese James Wang, engaged by the Royal Thai Government to survey existing farm economic conditions in Kalasin Province, Northeast Thailand, prior to their establishing a Government pilot farm project. This revealed the extent to which clearing of land was still necessary before the farmer could employ more than simple hand tools or, in some instances, ox-ploughs, for crop production.

TABLE 3.1   *Average annual growth of agricultural production 1952/54–1967/69**

Country	Per cent per year
AFRICA	
Dahomey	1·4
Chad	1·7
Nigeria	1·8
Guinea, Rep. of	2·2
Ethiopia	2·9
Madagascar	3·1
Uganda	3·4
Somalia	3·5
Gambia	3·6
Kenya	3·7
Mozambique	3·7
Ghana	4·0
Rhodesia	4·1
Cameroun	4·2

TABLE 3.1—*continued*

Country	Per cent per year
AFRICA	
Senegal	4·2
Niger	4·3
Malawi	4·4
Sudan	5·2
Upper Volta	5·7
Ivory Coast	6·1
ASIA	
Yemen	0·3
Indonesia	1·8
Burma	2·2
India	2·4
Saudi Arabia	2·7
Ceylon (Sri Lanka)	3·0
Cambodia (Kmer Republic)	3·3
Philippines	3·5
Formosa (Taiwan)	3·9
Malaysia:	
West	4·2 ⎫
Sabah	3·4 ⎬
Sarawak	2·7 ⎭
Thailand	4·6
AMERICA CENTRAL	
Barbados	0·1
Cuba	0·2
Jamaica	2·5
El Salvador	4·0
Panama	4·0
Honduras	4·1
Costa Rica	4·3
Guatemala	4·8
Mexico	5·0
Nicaragua	5·4
TROPICAL SOUTH AMERICA	
Paraguay	2·5
Peru	2·5
Colombia	2·8
Guyana	3·0
Brazil	3·7
Bolivia	4·5
Venezuela	5·5
Ecuador	6·3

* These figures of production growth refer to crop and livestock production and are exclusive of fishery and forestry sectors.
SOURCE: *World Agriculture: The last quarter century, FAO, Rome, 1970.*

TABLE 3.2   *Some total population growth rates per cent per year*
1952/56–1965/67

Country	Per cent per year
AFRICA	
Uganda	2·5
ASIA	
Indonesia	2·4
Burma	2·2
India	2·3
Ceylon (Sri Lanka)	2·5
Philippines	3·6
Formosa (Taiwan)	3·4
Malaysia	3·0
Thailand	4·0
AMERICA CENTRAL	
Cuba	2·3
Jamaica	1·6
Panama	3·1
Honduras	3·2
Guatemala	3·1
Mexico	3·6
Nicaragua	3·0
TROPICAL SOUTH AMERICA	
Paraguay	2·7
Peru	2·2
Colombia	3·5
Brazil	3·1
Venezuela	4·0

Some estimates of growth of the labour force per cent per year 1965–1980

East Africa	1·8
Middle South Asia*	1·9
South East Asia†	2·4
America Central	3·3
Tropical South America	3·0

* Includes Sri Lanka, India, Iran and Pakistan.
† Includes Burma, Cambodia, Indonesia, Malaysia, the Philippines and Thailand.
SOURCES: Clark and Haswell (1970) p. 86; Turnham (1970) p. 34.

TABLE 3.3   *The constraint of partially cleared land to the adoption of improved methods of cultivation, Kalasin Province, Northeast Thailand*

No. of standing trees	4,001
Average no. trees per hectare	13
No. of stumps still to be uprooted	11,261
Average no. stumps per hectare	37
No. of ant hills	1,389
Average no. of ant hills per hectare	5
Average no. of obstructions of all types per hectare	55
No. of farms surveyed	115
Total cultivated area (hectares)	307
Average size of farm (hectares)	2·67
Average no. of obstructions per farm	147
Total no. of plots	3,408
Average no. of plots per farm	29·6
Average hectares per plot	0·09

SOURCE: Unpublished data kindly made available by James Wang.

5. Jungle clearings in South-east Asia by means of fire.

6. Partially cleared land in Northeast Thailand showing standing trees and stumps still to be uprooted.

TABLE 3.4   *The 'six hands of farming': a proposition*

'Hand'	*Practice*
1.	Shifting cultivation slash-and-burn: the most primitive form of agriculture
2.	A proportion of trees, some ant hills, and the need to clear before draft animals can be used
3.	The use of draft animals
4.	The use of water requiring a network of dykes and ditches
5.	The use of fertiliser and insecticides
6.	Farmers follow modernised practices, including the use of mechanical equipment and hired labour, and produce entirely for the market

It is in this context that the 'six hands of farming' can most appropriately be formalised, before we embark on a study of the length and severity of periods between each 'hand', and the influences upon them of such factors as climate, population, institutional structure, and communications.

Surprisingly, the pre-agricultural primitive hunter and food-gatherer (no longer existing in great numbers) has at times needed a space requirement giving him something like a fortyfold margin over his consumption requirements.

Under the near arid conditions of the Kalahari, for example, where there is nothing but damp sand from which to procure water – skilfully sucked through a hollow reed and transferred for storage to ostrich egg shells – density of population is as low as 300 sq km per person.

7. Newly cleared land in southern Philippines littered with obstructions of all types.

8. All obstructions removed to make it possible to plough with draught animals.

Skilful though primitive hunters have been in tracking large animals, they often have to work hard hunting over extensive areas actually to kill them. Then there is the important fact that when they do catch a large animal they have no means of preserving it and much of the meat is bound to be wasted.

Sachs and Glees (1967) have estimated the stock of nine wild potential meat animals in an area of 30,000 sq km in the Serengeti, Tanzania. The Serengeti area is described as semi-arid, not capable of being grazed by cattle because of tsetse-fly infestation. The principal meat animals are wildebeest, Thompson gazelle and zebra. The live weight stock of meat animals is estimated at 4·3 tons per sq km with a ratio of meat and edible offal to live weight calculated to be 43 per cent. The authors estimate the possible annual rate of slaughter at only 10 per cent of the stock, however, which suggests that most of the game is eaten by wild predatory animals.

Holmberg (1950) records for a group of semi-nomadic hunters and food-gatherers inhabiting an extensive tropical area of eastern Bolivia that when food is plentiful people eat to excess and do little else; but when food is scarce they go hungry while looking for something more to eat. The supply of food is rarely abundant and always insecure.

It is against this background which, until relatively recently, extended over a millennium of time, that Clark and Haswell (1970) point out the effects of high mortality rates due to accidents in the hunting field, and the inability of such communities to give any support to ill or infirm people, which account for a rate of population growth which was almost negligibly slow – 'had it not been, the world would have passed through the hunting and fishing stage, and reached the agricultural stage, far quicker than it in fact did'.

Turning now to the most primitive type of agriculture – the actual cultivation of plants as opposed to the collection of naturally growing produce – we no longer think of population densities in such spacious terms as square kilometres per person, but begin to reverse the process.

Countrywise population densities shown in Table 2.1. cannot be regarded as a reliable index of the varying stages at which the several countries of the tropics are probably operating within the broad framework of the 'six hands of farming'. On such a scale, our frame of reference must be distribution of population rather than mean density. A fairly high population density within a country may also have large areas which are virtually unpopulated for a variety of reasons – for example, unfavourable climate, remoteness, tsetse fly, forest reserves – and the population may concentrate in more favourable areas.

Nonetheless, certain of the African and the tropical South American countries which have extremely low population densities ranging from one to ten persons per square kilometre, would seem by definition to have very large tracts of land in which many of their peoples still practise the most primitive type of agriculture of all – that of shifting cultivation by slash-and-burn methods.

Even in Asia we still find quite extensive areas of what Pelzer (1954) describes as 'an economy of which the main characteristics are rotation of fields rather than crops; clearing by means of fire; absence of draft animals and of manuring; use of human labour only; employment of the dibble stick or hoe; short periods of soil occupancy alternating with long fallow periods'.

But, as he points out, just as advanced agriculture does not depend on the animal-drawn plough, primitive agriculture does not depend on the hoe. A more fundamental distinction may be made in terms of land use. Shifting cultivators clear with axes and hand knives preferably virgin forest (leaving the stumps of large trees scattered over the area), burn the brushwood, and raise a crop generally for one, two or three years in succession, after which the land is rested for a varying number of years.

Peters (1950), for example, found the Lala shifting cultivators, growing finger millet on poor soils in Zambia, operating an average cycle of seventeen years; the writer found a region in Gambia in which shifting cultivation (now abandoned) could only be operated on a twenty-year cycle on soils which were exceptionally poor.

Similarly, Freeman (1955) observed the Iban in Sarawak resting land after taking one or two crops for a period as long as twenty years where soils were poor but only ten years where soils were 'good'. Conklin's (1957) findings for a small upland group of shifting cultivators on the island of Mindoro in the Philippines, which has a tropical monsoon climate, abundant rainfall, and a lush vegetation, were that the average cycle lasted twelve years of which two to four were cultivated and the remainder fallow.

Milpa cultivation (swidden) in Central America has the same sort of cycle as in Asia. In the Shan Hills (Burma) a fifteen year cycle was recognised; Rhind recalls that shorter periods arose either through population pressure or because of tribal wars.

Intercountry comparisons of population densities can thus be misleading. Though Peters in Africa estimated that soil deterioration might begin when population density rose higher than two persons per square kilometre, Freeman in Malaysia calculated that there was a danger of land deterioration when the ratio rose above 20 persons per square kilometre; Conklin computes an even higher figure of the maximum population capacity of the land in his Mindoro sample of *swidden* (slash-and-burn) cultivators of 39 persons per square kilometre.

It is in Mindanao, however, the southernmost and second largest island of the Philippines that the writer obtained data which enables us to quantify in terms of rising land prices from a base year of initial land clearing, the relative importance of the first four 'hands of farming'.

Almost half of the land surface area of the Philippines is afforested; much of this is accounted for in Mindanao with many areas of climax forest, or mature second growth forest, containing sparse populations practising slash-and-burn cultivation. Into this region settlers have been encouraged to move in the past few decades to relieve densely populated areas in other regions of the country.

In selecting a site for settlement, it is important to note that if it contains any productive tree crops (jackfruit, betel nut, banana, coconut, for example), even if the forest has not been cut down for several decades, the original planter may and invariably does demand payment for these, as they will be destroyed by fire in reclearing the plot. Otherwise, land is regarded as a 'free good'.

This is confirmed by Conklin in his study of Hanunoo agriculture. He found payments being made to the original planter – 'permissible though not highly approved' – and makes the vital points, to which we will refer again later, that 'tenure is by usufruct only' and 'all cultivates are privately owned as long as they remain productive'.

Table 3.5 records the actual situation in a mature second growth forest area of Mindanao. (Conklin (p. 41) states for his Mindoro sample that 'in general, mature second growth forest is considered better *swidden* site vegetation than primary forest because the latter is more difficult to cut, takes longer to dry out after cutting, rarely burns completely, and thus requires more labour'.)

Land values have been converted into paddy equivalents, the preferred staple foodgrain of the area, from price data which indicate that prices of paddy paid to the peasant producer in so far as he has had a marketable surplus over home consumption needs, have remained virtually unchanged over the seventeen-year period. Added to this somewhat surprising factor is the 'plateau' which appears to be sustained following the sharp rise in the price of land after initial clearing, with relatively little change in land values even when water is made available for crop production by a simple system of dyke and ditch networks.

TABLE 3.5 *An example of progression over time from slash-and-burn axe agriculture to the use of water for irrigation*

'Hand'	Practice	Land value average price/ha m. tons paddy equivalent	Interval years
1.	Shifting cultivation: payment to original planter for a few productive trees in dense second growth forest	0·09	
2.	Partial clearance: some trees and stumps scattered over site	0·26	2
3.	Use of draft animals: land almost entirely cleared of trees and stumps	1·18	5
	Land entirely free from trees and stumps	2·12	13
4.	Gravity flow irrigation using dykes and ditches	3·53	17

TABLE 3.6   *Rise in the price of land per cent per year from initial clearing to potential use under irrigation*

First seven years	Hand 1 and 2	43·5		
Next six years	Hand 3	10·4		
Next four years	Hand 3 – 'dry' area suitable for irrigation as defined in Hand 4 which became available in year seventeen	13·6	11·6	23·8

Two factors emerge as dominant requirements if rates of growth of agricultural production are to be accelerated. Firstly, that if water for irrigation is a high priority in narrowing the time factor in the development process, roads have an even higher priority; for this area remains to this day undeveloped in transport and communication networks which keeps producer prices low and offers no incentive to apply additional labour and adopt new techniques with the use of water for crop production.

And secondly, the rural community concerned had been exposed to pressure of population by a substantial net migration over natural increase; otherwise, it would have taken much longer to reach the present stage of agricultural development in which a tillage system is practised within the broad definition given by Duckham and Masefield (1970) of 75 per cent or more of the ploughable land being under tillage crops or one year fallow.

In so far as inducement to acceleration of agricultural development is proposed by encouraging a substantial inflow of peoples from elsewhere, without a proper understanding of land rights and social and economic structures of the 'traditional' environment, conflicts and 'political' disturbances are likely to arise which could prove too high a price to pay in initial stages.

Much depends on land tenure as soon as there is settled agriculture. If there is clear legal registration of title as in most of India and Burma then fragmentation is automatically adjusted by the sale of uneconomic fields and amalgamation of split holdings. If title is uncertain land is scarcely saleable because buyers cannot be sure who is the rightful owner and in these circumstances fragmentation can reach absurd results; the tatu-maru system in Sri Lanka is a well-known example where land is rotated in time between joint owners when the holding becomes too small. It is common for a man to farm a field once in ten or more years (Rhind *in lit.*).

A tale is told of a lawsuit over a 480th part of the produce of one coconut palm. (The yield of a palm/year would be good at 100 nuts.)

CHAPTER 4

Discontinuities: Causes and Consequences

*In the forest areas innumerable bush paths lead
from compound to compound, village to village.
These paths have been maintained through the
years by the tread of feet*

F. J. Pedler (1955)

A young ex-farm institute trainee in East Malaysia enthusiastically set about cultivating a garden plot, digging a fish pond, and building a piggery, on an 'acre' of land adjacent to a gravel road. The village community to which he belonged had recently moved from the riverside to the roadside because they said when the people were far from the road they had to carry everything on their backs, and this is hard work.

But after this initial burst of innovation and activity, the young man grew despondent, for the road had been completed five years earlier and 'still no hawker is travelling up and down to buy things'. The young man's dilemma was that he had become market-oriented, but was trying to operate in a population vacuum. Of itself, the road offered no inducement to accelerate agricultural development; it generated no new traffic but merely linked two points of minor urban concentration at high initial cost. It traversed an extensive area still under slash-and-burn shifting cultivation in a thinly populated region in which the inhabitants produced virtually all they required for home consumption. This poses a situation in which markets are so distant as to lead to prohibitive transport costs.

If no inflow of population occurs and the area remains dependent on natural increase, then Johnston's much longer time scale in reaching a 'structural transformation turning point' may prevail; and the young man's dilemma will be that the acquisition of new techniques through training, only to return to the traditional scene of his birth and childhood, leaves him ahead of his time within this extremely narrow context of his social and economic environment. There is no pressure of population; the first 'Hand' of farming hangs on; government administrations and development planners become more and more exasperated.

Faced with this frontier of traditional agriculture, we may safely assume with Ester Boserup (1965) that communities living under a long fallow system will only go in for changes 'under the compulsion of increasing population or under the compulsion of a social hierarchy'.

In the previous chapter we ended with the second condition present in a southern Philippine settlement, which had progressed in under two decades from shifting cultivation to the use of water for crop production. And who can blame the economist who allows himself to make such glib statements as 'a new equilibrium point has been reached'?

Table 4.1 partially refutes this conclusion for, in terms of producer price, the immigrant who opens up an area of mature second-growth forest is no more favourably placed after seventeen years of 'taming' that forest than is the ex-trainee returning to his forest homeland who attempts to modernise in an area isolated by low population densities which permit the continued practice of slash-and-burn agriculture to go unchecked. Both situations represent what might more precisely be called a point of discontinuity.

TABLE 4.1   *Index numbers of average producer price received by immigrants opening up new land compared with that received by permanent tillage farmers in more developed regions of the Philippines*

	Land resettled by immigrants	Intensively cultivated land in permanent tillage in evacuated areas
1953 producer price (paddy) = 100		
Year 1–1953	100	244
Year 17–1970	100	401
		Percentage change
		165

What keeps producer prices low? Mindanao has the most favourable climate of the country; it is virtually outside the typhoon belt; much of the area is still covered by forest; large tracts of land are still open to settlement.

The index numbers are a measure of the inability of the settler who grows paddy on newly cleared second-growth forest to command a price as high as that received by producers operating on permanent tillage in other regions; though it should not be overlooked that this price difference may contain a significant element of quality difference. Varieties suitable for slash-and-burn (Kaingin) culture have inferior grain from those grown on permanent flooded rice lands; they invariably mill poorly with higher breakage rates, and cook to a sticky consistency.

What is surprising, in a country which has been a net importer of rice, however, is that for over a decade, despite the efforts of immigrants who have brought new land under permanent tillage, there has been no significant variation in average producer price over the years, though seasonal variations follow a familiar pattern. What are the factors which have led to a situation in which settlers continue to accept low product prices from year to year? Is it sufficient to assume that they are mainly concerned with established food crops for home consumption, and that they lack responsiveness to economic opportunity?

The 'discontinuity' in the price of land after sharp increases with initial clearing shown in Table 3.6 has been interpreted as a function of transport and communications. Horst von Oppenfeld (1957) and his associates refer to the 'extreme low' in land values in Mindanao compared with other regions in 1954–55. In Mindanao 'much land is still undeveloped. Settlers can aquire homesteads or land in organised settlements of the National Resettlement and Rehabilitation Administration free of charge.'

The wide range in land values in various regions of the country they attribute mainly to geographic location, productivity, and relative availability of arable land. 'Mindanao, where settlers can still acquire land free of charge, has the highest proportion of owner-operators.'

If we concede the principle that the price of land, once cleared, is a consequence of its rent, the absence of tenants should be added to the list of possible causes of discontinuity. In a South Indian study (Haswell, 1967), it was found that highest rents were paid where tenants had nowhere else to go; as soon as there was competition for their labour in local industry, tenants were only forthcoming at a very low rental with a consequent fall in the price of land.

On the other hand, where landowners feel that their political future is secure, they may bid land up to very high prices.

> Landowners can feel political stability in communist Yugoslavia where private ownership of small farms is permitted, and the price of land in the most densely populated region is about as high as anywhere in the world. ... In sparsely populated, newly settled countries, on the other hand, such as Brazil, the prices of land measured in real terms are low. ... The comparatively low prices of land in pre-communist China probably measure the effect of political insecurity, largely counteracting the effects of high rural population density and lack of alternative employment, which would have been expected to raise prices (Jacoby, 1971).

It is this last factor which operates in the settlements of certain areas in Mindanao where political insecurity keeps product prices low, and leads to discontinuities which leave a wide open field for the 'occasional' entrant to a market to exploit the situation; although such an entrant may engage in petty trading and the collection of loans at high interest rates in terms of kind payments at harvest, he operates within a very narrow confine, buying from local farmers in one season and selling back to them in another. His ability to gain a large measure of control over a population is, in this context, a function of relative isolation from good transport networks.

But the security factor dominates: when land has been cleared entirely of trees and stumps and a permanent system of tillage has been established, the original planter or his descendants even though they may not have cut down that particular forest for several decades before the arrival of the settlers, returns to claim the land if necessary by force – recalling conveniently that under primitive structures 'tenure is by usufruct only'. Many panic, sell standing crops at low prices, and vanish for a time or for ever.

The producer operating in areas of sparse populations and new settlements can neither look behind him for the security he requires, nor ahead for the links which connect him with sizeable market towns and offer him an incentive to increase agricultural production.

Von Oppenfeld (1957) shows that 'in the newly settled areas of Mindanao where transportation facilities are often inadequate, the distances of the farm from the nearest market had a marked effect on land valuation'.

If land values are held at an 'extreme low' because 'much land is still undeveloped', the side benefits of ribbon development in which point-to-point lines and super-highways may have no feeder transport will be few. Developments will exist only as 'isolated beads strung on the line'; not only do we find the price of land from its already 'extreme low' falling further as holdings are situated further and further from the roadside, but, under these conditions, product fed to points on a ribbon development main highway will be by high-cost porterage, ox-sled, or ox-cart.

The cost of 'off-line' transport by porterage is prohibitive at a distance of 7 km from the local market because as much as half of the gross product will have to be expended in order to get one ton kilometre of transport performed; by ox-sled this would consume only one-fifth of the gross product at a distance of 7 km, but such a distance is beyond the range of ox-sled performance. A much cheaper form of transport is the ox-cart because greater loads can be carried, thereby reducing the proportion of gross product required to get one ton kilometre of transport performed to one-tenth.

Primary dependence even on the bullock cart imposes crippling spatial limitations upon the economy, however. In India, bullocks are

TABLE 4.2   *The effect of distance from market on the price of land in permanent tillage after clearing and with access to water*

Distance to market km   *Land value in paddy*   *Price Index*
                            equivalents: 1954—55   *(highest = 100)*
                            m ton/ha

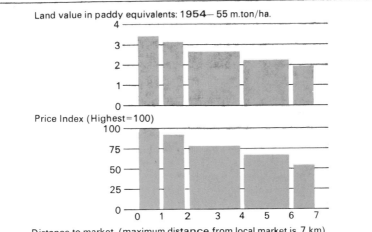

Land value in paddy equivalents: 1954—55 m.ton/ha.

Price Index (Highest=100)

Distance to market (maximum distance from local market is 7 km)

9. Ribbon development in West Africa where a super-highway has no feeder transport links.

10. High-cost porterage in South-east Asia where feeder roads and bridges are
unfit for wheeled transport.

still the backbone of the agricultural economy of the country,
providing both agricultural and rural transport services; here, the
economic limit is reached with ox-cart transport at a distance of
11 km from the market and transport costs by this means are found
to be prohibitive at greater distances (Haswell 1967). Significantly,
this is a transport cost at about the 12 per cent level, and refers to the
transportation of a crop grown for cash, namely sugar. However,
Rhind points out from experience of Burma that, in Burma, the
economic limit for ox cart travel on an average country road in dry
weather was found to be 20 km; but Burma carts are lighter than
Indian carts, and do not carry such a heavy load – 200–250 kg
dependent on gradient. Greater distances can be covered, but the oxen

11. Transporting product in West Africa to a main highway first up-stream by canoe then transferring to a bullock cart.

need a full day's rest to recuperate – travelling on a down gradient being the more arduous.

Indeed, in Mountain Province in the Philippines' largest island of Luzon in the north, vegetable producers will not grow at distances greater than 1·6 km from the roadside pick-up point because of the high cost in time and labour in carrying cabbages by shoulder up steep slopes.

Although porterage is a contributory factor affecting the price of agricultural land, the proportionate differences in the decline in land values between producers who have access to a sizeable urban market for vegetables and those in sparsely populated regions is very considerable.

Clark and Haswell (1970, p. 192) quote the Ministry of National Economy in Madagascar as having observed in an analysis of the price structure for certain crops the undesirable effects of transport difficulties which, under certain circumstances, drives poor farmers deeply into debt and to the pledging of future crops at 'derisory' prices. That this largely neglected state of affairs, and the discontinuities which it reflects, represents one of the gravest threats to 'political' security and economic development, has now become increasingly evident. The seriousness of the situation is all the more apparent when we take account of the millions of cultivators upon whom it imposes a low-income constraint.

12. An ox-sled in southern Philippines taking produce to the buying point on the main highway.

The high proportion of ox-sled and buffalo's back transport in von Oppenfeld's Mindanao survey sample shown below – a high cost method of transport – helps to keep the price of land low in 'off-line' areas; of greater significance is that although 14 per cent of his Mindanao sample could be reached by truck in 1954, by 1970 land values in tillage areas with access to motorable roads continued to be at an 'extreme low' despite increased use of trucks. More importantly, farmers who sell marketable surpluses of paddy or maize to primary buyers use motor vehicles provided by the buyer who invariably pays a 'derisory' price to the producer which bears no relationship to market prices – ostensibly and sometimes justifiably to 'compensate' him for bad road conditions, 'earth' roads which are slippery, full of potholes, and roads which are at times impassable prohibiting the use

TABLE 4.3   *Land value at market prices in m. tons paddy equivalent: Philippines*

	per ha.	Price Index (Highest = 100)
Mountain Province (Luzon)		
Land adjacent to super-highway within 7km distance from an urban city comprising a population between 50,000 and 100,000	122·2–85·5	100–70
One to two kilometers back from the roadside	29·3–24·4	24–20
Sparsely populated Provinces of Mindanao		
Tillage areas with access to motorable roads	3·6–2·4	3–2
'Off-line' areas with no feeder transport	0·24	0·02

SOURCE: Haswell (1970) p. 59.

TABLE 4.4   *Method of transportation of farm produce for short distances to primary buyer or local market*

	Philippines: 1954–55	
	Central Luzon	Mindanao
	%	%
Truck	64	14
Jeep	7	–
Two-wheeled horse-drawn vehicle	5	–
Train	–*	–
Ox-cart	16	–
Ox-sled	2	44
Buffalo's back	1	28
Men's shoulder	1	2
	96	88
Other	4	12
	100	100

* Less than 0·5 per cent.
SOURCE: von Oppenfeld *et al.* (1957) p. 132.

of large vehicles and causing even 3 to 5 ton capacity trucks to incur heavy maintenance costs.

Low producer prices, however, are not always solely a function of high 'off-line' transport costs incurred by primary buyers who provide trucks where road conditions are poor; traditional practices, poor yields, and low prices, form a vicious circle which compels many peasant producers to borrow for food during the cultivating season – a period of worsening stocks and highest work load and energy requirements – on condition of repayment at the time of harvest.

In these circumstances, primary buyers in a given locality may not only be the main buyers, but also the isolated entrants to a market who have a vested interest in making such loans and collecting the kind payment literally off the threshing floor.

CHAPTER 5

Production Requirements: Early Stages of Agricultural Development

A small, closed farming community turns over the available nutrients with little loss or little gain, but even in a small human community there is always a tendency to concentrate fertility near the homestead ... and there arises an area of high fertility. ...

J. B. Hutchinson (1969)

'Because of the heavy pressure of population the majority of agricultural holdings in the Philippines are extremely small.' This extraordinary statement appears in an appendix in Jacoby's *Man and Land* (1971). The compiler of this appendix, Amanuens Leif Stahl, seems to have stumbled into the trap of using aggregate figures at the national level, and then proceeded to prove his thesis by a breakdown of conditions in rural areas centred on the multimillion capital city – the point of maximum polarisation of the population without reference to the considerable areas with population densities of twenty persons or lower per square kilometre.

Even in India, universally stated as most densely populated, cut-and-burn shifting agriculture still persists over quite extensive tracts where population is so sparse as to permit its regular practice. More pertinently, Hutchinson (1969) reminds us that 'the study of land deterioration is a recent one, and those who first enquired into it were so impressed with the damage that has resulted from erosion and salination that there arose a belief that land once lost was lost forever, and the basic resources available to mankind were being permanently depleted'. Indeed, erosion may not always lead to damage in the long run – consider the great rice bowls of Asia, flood plains of the Irrawaddy, Ganges, Mekong, and the Yellow River, all of which are the result of erosion or the moving of soil from poor mountain areas to where it can be much more productive, supporting quite dense populations.

Much confusion arises from the prevailing tendency to project for countries as a whole a set of conditions which are a phenomenon belonging strictly to congested urban peripheries. Preoccupation with this phenomenon, the unprecedented ruralisation of urban cities and their environs, has led to a serious neglect of that tough hard core of this growing problem of modernisation without development – the mushroom growth of towns which are no more than trading centres generating debt.

Clark and Haswell refer to the need clearly to distinguish between the area of land which a man 'requires' to produce his subsistence, and that which he would like to have if he is to earn an economic living; only if the amount of land actually available falls short of 'requirements' may we legitimately state the case for 'rural overpopulation' or 'underemployment'.

But the amount of labour which can be economically expended on a given area of land varies greatly both with the crops cultivated and the agricultural methods available, which in turn are dependent on man's ability to control the three major variable components of the natural environment of agriculture – energy, water, and soil. These are succinctly summarised by Hutchinson (1969):

Man has no control, and no prospect of control, over the incidence of solar radiation, and the pattern of distribution of temperature and day length over the world is one which must be accepted as we find it . . . over water supplies man gained a measure of control early in the history of agriculture, in that he learnt how to supplement by irrigation from rivers the inadequacy of the rainfall in arid lands . . . given adequate water supplies and suitable temperatures, agricultural productivity depends upon the fertility of the soil. Soil is a living system, distinguished from the geological formations beneath by the living flux of growth and decay in plant roots, surface debris, and the soil-inhabiting animals, fungi and bacteria. Its inorganic materials are of geological origin, but its structure, and performance as a nutrient medium for plants, is determined by the climate of the region and the vegetation that grows upon it.

We shall first seek to answer the general question of how much land an agricultural population 'requires' to produce its subsistence by traditional methods of cultivation.

A convenient unit of measurement for determining at what level of population density it can be said that land is overpopulated in an agricultural sense is the number of hectares of cultivated land per adult male engaged in agriculture. For most low income economies with their higher proportion of children in the population, the number of males engaged in agricultural work may be taken as one quarter of the whole, after making allowance for village craftsmen and traders. This is substantiated by direct measurement for the sparsely populated provinces of Mindanao in southern Philippines in which the proportion of adult males engaged in agriculture was found to be 25·2 per cent. Table 5.1 illustrates the relevance of this measure in a comparison of land/man ratios under varying conditions of population density, and of agricultural practice in the sense described by Takase and Kano (1969) that merely of cultivating 'land' under rainfed conditions or under conditions where 'water control' is possible – but preceding the 'inputs' period and the 'culti-methods' period.

Effectively, we can leave aside the 'first hand' of farming, that of shifting cultivation, the most primitive form of agriculture, in the present context of what a man 'requires' to produce his subsistence;

TABLE 5.1 *Land/man ratios as a theoretical determinant of 'requirement' for subsistence production**

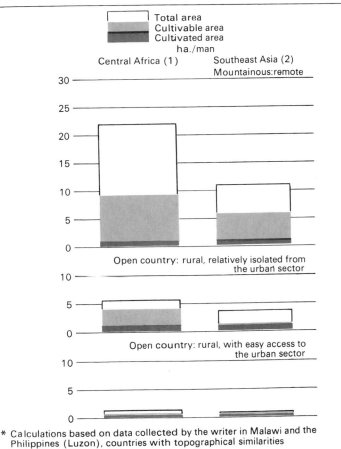

* Calculations based on data collected by the writer in Malawi and the Philippines (Luzon), countries with topographical similarities

(1) Single cropping of maize (2) Multiple cropping: paddy and maize

for the current pressures of rising expectations invalidate measurements of the customary level of production at which precontact subsistence agriculture communities aim.

Empirical studies indeed show that bands of peoples living by slash-and-burn methods – the cultivation of an area for one, two, or three years in succession, followed by long periods of regeneration up to thirty years or more – aim at a production which ranges from 220 to 250 kg of whole grain per person per year, dependent on the type of grain grown and expected losses from hand-pounding to remove indigestible outer layers. These may vary from about 10 per cent or less for millets to 30 per cent or more for rice.

This we find to be the demand ceiling, under conditions in which communities subsisting in a precontact economy have no incentive to produce beyond their customary and immediate consumption needs, although these may be well below their capacity to produce. We shall examine more closely the tropical forest areas which continue to afford shelter to such communities when we come to analyse some of the effects of deliberate policies to resettle peoples from more densely populated areas.

It is the preoccupation with producing what is 'required' for subsistence of farm-family households falling within the second, third, and fourth 'hand' of farming that constitutes the main area of darkness and unpredictability, since this level of farming is practised by the majority of those masses who live in the rural sector of low income countries which have overwhelmingly large proportions of their population in agriculture. Even though resources may be utilised for those products which are 'required' for subsistence, within this range of agricultural practice farm-family households 'require' some cash both as production units and as consumption units, because they are exposed to the exchange economy.

Given a land abundant situation however, Table 5.1 indicates that households tend towards expansion of operation up to a point averaging about 2 hectares per adult male worker engaged in agriculture – rather less in mountainous terrain where cultivation is arduous because of steep slopes.

Data for 1970–71 from a survey in southern Philippines in which farm-family households practise multiple cropping of rice and maize under rainfed conditions and without application of industrial inputs, indicates that the amount of land 'required' for subsistence is 1·88 hectares per adult male engaged in agriculture.

Hoffman (1967) calculated from case studies of progressive farmers in central Malawi that an area of at least 0·3035 ha per *person* should be set aside for home consumption unless yields of maize of more than 1350 kg per ha can be expected continuously. This implies that the cultivator must devote 1·2 ha per adult male engaged in agriculture to produce what is 'required' for home consumption; only if multiple cropping is practised, as is sometimes possible in the South-east Asian example given in Table 5.1, can this be reduced to about 0·9 hectares per adult male engaged in agriculture. Hoffman's estimate makes allowance for seed requirements, and 25 per cent on-farm storage losses of maize (which was found to be of this order of magnitude independently by the writer during a survey of crop damage by rat and insect pest infestation).

This leaves those households in the pre-'inputs' stage under the particular African conditions of single cropping of maize unlikely to be able to provide all they 'require' for their subsistence at densities of 0·8 ha cultivated area per adult male engaged in agriculture, while those households in South-east Asia who are multiple cropping are extremely insecure in the provision of what they 'require' for their subsistence at this density, because of the low yields which obtain.

Hoffman's estimate suggests a 'safety margin' in 410 kg maize per person per year based on a yield of 1,350 kg per hectare. A re-survey of a Gambia village in 1961–62 illustrates how near the margin for subsistence agricultural production was in some compounds (Haswell, 1963); total product ranged widely from 101 to 438 kg milled rice equivalent (converting other products at the rate at which they exchanged against milled rice in the local market) per person per year. In an earlier study of the same village in Gambia (Haswell, 1953), the proportion of adult males who were farming to total population was as high as 31·5 per cent, and the area cultivated in a relatively land abundant situation 1·67 hectares per adult male engaged in agriculture.

Clark and Haswell (1970) employ the de Vries generalisation about the early stages of agricultural progress in which all measurements are made in kilograms of unmilled grain equivalent/total population/year. E. de Vries was for some years Rector of the School of Social Studies in The Hague, and had previously worked for many years in Indonesia. According to his generalisation, the true subsistence minimum stands a little below 300 kg grain equivalent/person/year – a level of production which strictly belongs to the 'first hand' of farming. 'As production increases, perhaps to a level of 350, most of the increased product, not unexpectedly, is used to improve the diet,' Clark and Haswell point out.

> Even under these circumstances, however, a certain proportion of the crop has to be set aside for the purchase of a few necessary non-food commodities, payment of taxes, etc. By the time a production per head of 400 units has been reached, however, the community is selling a substantial part of its agricultural product – this indicates, in effect, the urgency of

other needs besides food, for clothing, building materials, medicines, and so forth. . . . Not until 500 units have been reached is it worth while employing animal rather than human labour.

It is the 300 to 500 kg grain equivalent/person/year category of producers which suffers the gravest financial and organisational constraints to increased production from agriculture. These are the subsistence cultivators of the second, third, and fourth 'hand' of farming; many millions of producers do in fact employ animal labour for which they cannot afford the necessary feed grain; neither should the selling of a substantial part of the agricultural product be considered as a market-oriented activity on the part of the producer.

Tanaka (1963) describes farmers' decisions as to a large extent determined by the marketing ratio or proportion of cash receipts through marketing to value of output of farm products. Marketing ratio he defines as 'an indicator which shows the object for which farm households are producing farm products'. He postulates that when a farm household's marketing ratio is above 80 per cent, it can be said that it is producing for sale. But when a farm household's marketing ratio is below 40 per cent it can be said it is producing for home consumption. He relates marketing ratio to size of holding, and estimates for Japanese farm households that farmers on arable holdings of less than 0·5 ha produce generally for home consumption, while those with more than 1 ha are market-oriented.

The foregoing assessment of farmers' decisions as to the amount of land they would like to cultivate to meet their home consumption needs of 2 ha/adult male engaged in agriculture, can be equated with Tanaka's 0·5 ha arable holding on the assumption that adult males so engaged represent one-quarter of the total population. Because this activity occupies such a large proportion of the population of the tropical world, there is a call for rigorous critical analysis of the causes of the low levels of agricultural productivity which are implied.

For these are conditions in which the real problem is not the incidence of cut-and-burn methods of cultivation, but poverty.

CHAPTER 6

The Services Apparatus and Economic Development

The peasant, because of the multiplicity of diseases
to which he is exposed and which sap his energy, is
often an inefficient agriculturist; because he is
undernourished he is more susceptible to the wide
range of diseases to which he is exposed

R. M. Buchanan and J. G. Pugh (1955)

Colin Clark, in co-authorship with myself (1970), refers to a regression which appears to have been taking place in the early nineteenth century in a community in the Scottish highlands of which his grandfather was a member. 'Increasing population density, higher rents, and lower prices for their produce, meant that crofters in some of the poorer districts were unable to afford even ox ploughs, and reverted to hand cultivation. It was estimated that a man could dig 2 ha in the months January to April.'

The hand digging of 2 ha in the Scottish highlands cannot be equated with the situation of the farmer living in the tropics, however, who appears to seek and actually cultivate under certain conditions an area of about 2 ha, using hand hoes, or with the help of oxen.

The time factor for some operations in the tropics is vital to the establishment of a crop. Duckham and Masefield (1970) pinpoint this constraint:

In the tropics, theoretical environmental possibilities for plant growth often cannot be fully exploited because a perfect 'fit' of cropping plan to climate cannot be obtained for natural or economic reasons. Thus it is impossible to plant all crops exactly at the beginning of the rainy season when they would derive benefit from it, both because the soil may have been too hard to cultivate in the preceding dry season and precious weeks have to be wasted in this operation (after the rains have started), and because so much simultaneous planting makes an impossible demand on labour resources.

Again, with a single wet season of, say, five months, and a choice of crops each of which matures in three or four months, the planting of any of these crops will 'waste' one or two months of useful rain, which is, however, too short a period in which to mature a second crop.

Even in a single wet season two crops are sometimes possible, however; for example, early (90-day) sesamum followed by beans planted on late rains, a common combination in Burma (Rhind, *in lit.*). The beans are deep-rooted and tap water lower in the soil profile than the shallow-rooted sesamum. Nevertheless it is true that early sowing greatly enhances yields because of the flush of nitrates released in the soil with the first rains, which are subsequently leached down beyond reach of young crops.

A short wet season in which a badly distributed rain falls, and a long dry season with its hot dry conditions, immediately imposes a limit on the range of suitable crops. The variability and poor distribution of rainfall reduces the reliability of yields of even the suitable crops to a dangerously low level; and an early end to the rainy season can jeopardise the main harvest. Any one of these factors subjects the farmer to considerable risk when he is growing crops with a particular rainfall requirement.

Is there a kind of 'chicken-and-egg' relationship after all? Banks (1969) believes so in summing up one of the most deepseated problems of human communities, and one which is still far from solved in the tropical world: 'The conditions responsible for famine, for example, devastation by drought, flood, military action, or disease of plants and animals, [lead] to the overcrowded and insanitary conditions which predispose to pestilence, while the disruption, depopulation, inertia and fatalism following the latter [result] in failure to sow or harvest.' Such catastrophes are by no means things of the past. 'The security of the world from famine [in the 1960s] has depended on storage made possible by the wealth of the United States,' Hutchinson (1969) writes and proceeds to warn that 'there is a need for explicit recognition and study of the problems involved in the provision of stocks against climatic uncertainty'.

But this is too simple a view of a gravely insidious problem which continues to eat its way into whole societies with a relentless inevitability – that of failures to improve standards of health and its consequent deleterious effects on the efficiency of agricultural production; yet a more efficient production of food is indispensable if the vicious circle of poverty is to be broken.

Failure on this front is in part a function of the isolation of rural areas from the services apparatus. Van Dusseldorp (1971) offers a classification of the various types of centres which are required if concentration is the starting point for the policy of establishing social and economic services in rural areas.

Data available for north-east Thailand starkly illustrates the catastrophes and constraints which face rural populations even in situations which may broadly be termed as acceptable according to

TABLE 6.1   *Types of centre in rural areas*

Type of centre	Other names often used	Size of population	Radius of action
Additional primary	Hamlet	1,500	2 km
Primary	Local centre, village	1,500–5,000	3–6 km
Secondary	Large village, small town	5,000–10,000	8–20 km
Tertiary	Town, city	10,000	20 km

SOURCE: Van Dusseldorp (1971), p. 131.

van Dusseldorp's classification, wherever they are not served by fast and efficient road networks between these types of centres. Indeed, van Dusseldorp does continue to lay down certain further guidelines on the clear assumption that only when the centres are easily accessible to the population is concentration of services justified, and therefore that the relationships between types of centres and types of roads are all important.

This leads us to examine one of the primary problems of rural isolation, the seasonal risk rut and, where rainfall is badly distributed, pressure of population on the water supply: '1·2 million rai (192,000 ha) of land cannot be used: it is a desert in the dry season and a lake in the rainy season.' This cry came from peasant producers in six affected provinces of north-east Thailand.

Thailand recognises three seasons: the cool season, the dry season, and the wet season. According to the 1970 registration data on population of municipalities, Nakhornratchsima (Korat) has a population in the 50,000 to 100,000 bracket. This city by comparison with the surrounding rural area has a water supply, electricity supply, better housing, better roads, better sanitation, and access to medical care services; but still it does not have adequate garbage collection. From the Public Health administrators' point of view, therefore, it is defined as little more than half the standard of an adequate city standard. Even only 5 km on a paved highway distant from Korat villages still lack comparable public services such as water supply, garbage collection, and seepage disposal; what they do have is schooling and electricity on equal terms with the city-dweller.

But the partly inaccessible villages depend solely on the condition of the feeder road; 'if the condition of the feeder road is good the distance over which they may be reached can be as far as 10 to 12 kilometres'.

This radius of action of a primary centre falls within van Dusseldorp's secondary centre concentration of service units – proposed for

Trengganu in West Malaysia on the east coast of the Malay Peninsular – which would be at a junction of tertiary roads and a secondary road serving a town population of 10,000 persons. The social facilities among the service functions proposed at the secondary centre include primary and secondary schools, a clinic, combined health centre and hospital, and postal agency. But the Korat example indicates that if the condition of the feeder road is bad even primary centres can only be reached up to 5 km away from the all-weather highway; as has been stated earlier, beyond this health conditions will be at their very worst compared to the urban area. This is borne out by van Dusseldorp's functions and characteristics of the several types of services centres in which the radius of action of the primary centre ranges from 3 to 6 km; but the social facilities in his model for a population to be served of from 1,500 to 5,000 persons dwindle to simply a clinic, a

13. Returning to the homestead after making a few essential purchases at the village store.

14. In Central Africa this family digs in dried out river beds in search for water.

primary school, police post, and postal agency – although the economic facilities proposed are quite extensive.

This fact has bred some of the greatest evils of two development decades in which small towns have emerged which can be described as no more than trading centres generating debt, for there has been a concentration in few hands of just those economic facilities which van Dusseldorp (1971) proposes – shops, a small market, a workshop/ pump station, storage facilities, and rural industries (rice mill) – to which peasant producers whose energy has been sapped and whose agriculture has become inefficient through exposure to acute and chronic diseases are prey in times of personal stress.

Chronic diseases are those which occur throughout all seasons, and their causes are placed in the following order of priority by health research workers in Thailand: climatic conditions, food habits, personal hygiene, and environmental sanitation. Dry season health hazards in the north-east are caused by lack of water, drinking contaminated water, and by dust; and diseases of the upper respiratory tract remain prevalent during the wet season.

The first in importance among the chronic diseases is tuberculosis. Banks (1969) refers to it as the 'captain of the men of death' and states that it continues to maintain an iron grip on the peoples of the developing countries, both in the slums of the rapidly growing cities and in the rural areas. Tuberculosis and the venereal diseases present the greatest problems of control . . . it is not always appreciated that many of the so-called 'tropical' diseases were at one time common also to the temperate zones. It is not merely a matter of a harsh physical environment, but of a combination of this with poverty, ignorance, bad housing, and faulty customs, habits and beliefs. Control of the great killing diseases by modern methods does not solve these basic factors, but may merely make it possible for more people to live longer under the same or worse conditions than before, with malnutrition and related diseases in place of famine and pestilence.

Traditional agricultural practice involves a number of operations which require different intensities of energy output or work; and for

15. Time and energy are lost in daily porterage of water through the long dry season of the Northeast of Thailand.

16. A large number of storage containers are indispensable items of expenditure for households ekeing out life-giving water through several months of drought.

certain operations cultivators are inclined to rest a great deal, as well as depending on division of labour between the sexes and by age groups to carry them through an agricultural cycle of activity. In a short wet single crop, long dry season situation, concentration of labour on agricultural operations will be confined to little more than half the year, but the debilitating effects of chronic disease leads not only to preoccupation with planting to meet home consumption needs, but also delayed planting.

Labour in the busy periods, soon after the rains begin and during the first weeding particularly, has opportunities of being much more productive than labour at other seasons. It is not only 'scarcity of season', however, that is overriding, but coupled with this the health status of farm-family operators – their ability to maintain sustained effort, the effect of chronic sickness on managerial capacity, the willing-ness to innovate and to take risks.

Under favourable climatic conditions in which crop production is possible throughout the year, we can largely eliminate 'scarcity of season'; but there has been much wastage of packages of inputs which have been drafted into such areas without reference to the health status of communities, and its effect on their ability to exploit the new inputs for higher levels of agricultural production.

For example, as Banks points out, the influence of malaria has been and remains important, not only as a major cause of premature death but the chronic ill-health that it produces,

which has profound effects on the growth of populations and on food production. The 'silent' nature of the disease and its lack of dramatic symptoms puts it in a similar category to other diseases caused by parasitic infestations, such as bilharzia and hookworm. The people chiefly affected do not recognise their serious nature nor can they afford the time for prolonged courses of treatment.

We have but to take the situation in Korat Province alone; one-quarter of the area is highly malarious in the wet season, just at the time of greatest energy requirements for agricultural production. About one-quarter of the whole population of the Province have malaria 'to a medium extent', about half are not affected since malaria-carrying mosquitoes 'cannot live in the plain or in the urban area', and the remainder may be acutely affected. Chronic sickness cannot be overlooked as a primary factor in the high leisure preference which peasant producers so frequently exhibit.

An old saying in Gambia is that 'early clearing, early planting, early weeding make a good crop'. And for the chronically sick, it makes sense to conserve labour by practising an extensive system of agriculture which gives a positive return per unit of labour input rather than intensify for higher returns per unit of area. But sickness, particularly when acute sickness falls at a crucial time in the agricul-tural cycle, may result in late clearing, late planting, or late weeding, with consequent reduction in crop yields.

The energy cost of many agricultural activities is metabolically severe. Measurements of total time in the field spent resting were recorded for different tasks in Gambia (Haswell, 1953) which confirm the general statement made by Philipps (1954) that 'no man is ever observed to continue for prolonged periods without rest'. He illustrates this point by reference to grass-cutting, one of several tasks performed by seven Nigerians used as subjects. Philipps found that grass-cutting consumed 269 calories per hour of continuous work; but at least half the day is spent resting or sharpening tools – thus the overall cost of grass-cutting is approximately 120 calories per hour, the equivalent of steady walking at 4·8 km (3 miles) per hour.

TABLE 6.2 *An estimate of the energy cost of some main agricultural tasks in hand-hoe agriculture*

Task	Duration	Time in field spent resting	Calorie consumption per hour of continuous work	Approximate energy cost allowing for time spent resting	Actual time expended on agricultural task as per cent of available time
	Days	%*	Cal/hr†	Cal/hr	%
Hoeing; pre-planting cultivation	21	42	274	159	9·5
Weeding and thinning	56	29	269	191	41·0
Lifting seedlings from seedbeds and transplanting (in the production of paddy)	28	24	218	165	60·7
Harvesting	42	9	184	167	95·2

* Based on Fox results (Haswell, 1953).   † Based on Philipps results (1954).

Table 6.2 indicates the resistance to undertaking the more arduous tasks in the earlier part of the new agricultural season, when stocks of food are usually low and prices are high for purchased foodgrains from local merchants, older members of the community are consciously conserving energy, and those in poor health are showing signs of lethargy. But it is these very tasks that must be performed early to secure the higher output, and for which any period of sudden acute disease can spell disaster, reducing a family to borrowing simply to buy food.

Later on in the season, for paddy production the greater amount of time expended on transplanting in particular is an imposition caused by the limited period during which this operation can be performed; this is a task which usually calls for additional labour, and is characterised by the organisation of work groups, exchange labour, hire of labour, and failing all these possibilities, loss of output caused by seasonal shortage of labour.

Harvesting is a relatively light task, but one which nevertheless is pursued with, at times, almost hysterical intensity to wrest as much of the grain as possible from predatory animals, from shattering, from 'thieving neighbours', and to deal with the uneven ripening which is a byproduct of poor drainage in some cases, or poor selection of seed, or just bad husbandry.

The farmer who has grown a marketable surplus must, where there are no transport facilities, headload or pay porters to headload, and is faced with costs which soon become prohibitive. In his sample of seven Nigerians, whose average body weight was 55 kg (about 7·5 stone), Philipps takes a walking value of 120 cal/hr as the zero point in determining the energy cost of porterage. 'It is evident', he states from his findings, 'that total energy expenditure increases linearly with the weight of head load carried only up to an optimum level which would appear to be at 20 kg. Any further increase in head load clearly leads to a disproportionate increase in energy cost.'

By comparison, the metabolic costs, for instance, of head panning 30 and 35 kg loads respectively 'an extra 33 cal is expended for an increase of only 5 kg head load; it is apparent that there is an optimum head load that will ensure maximum economy of performance and comfort'.

Even for the man who has escaped chronic or acute sickness, conditions at tropical temperatures are very different from those in temperate regions typical of the climate in the Scottish highlands where crofters in the early nineteenth century apparently reverted voluntarily to the arduous task of hand digging as a cheaper form of cultivation than the use of ox ploughs.

Trowell (1955) emphasises that 'many forms of physical activity may produce a feeling of discomfort long before it is possible to recognise "climatic stresses"', and adults and children 'may not find pleasure but discomfort in physical activity'.

Can it be said, however, that low productivity activity in agriculture is a result of inertia? Given well tried methods over many generations, the local farmer may be expected to exhibit a shrewd idea of the extent to which it pays him to adopt the modern methods presented to him – or indeed, within his very limited horizon and the relative security of known practices, he may deliberately decide to stick to the old ways. Such is the insecurity all about him that a small economic gain may not be worth having.

CHAPTER 7

The Phenomenon of the Low Labour-utilization Economy

The amount of labour available for farm work depends fundamentally on two factors, that is the number of members in the family who can work on the family farm and the length of time each family member is prepared to work on the family farm

D. W. Norman (1970)

In low-income agricultural regions of the tropics, there has been a tendency towards an equalisation among farms and areas of the average product rather than the marginal product of agricultural labour, in which the concept of average productivity has been seen as a function of the size of the labour force, and marginal productivity assumed to be zero when an increase in the labour force has not been accompanied by an increase in the labour input.

But marginal productivity must refer to the labour input, expressed in hours, days, or other convenient unit, of work actually performed, and not to the size of the available labour force whether or not it is at work.

In other words, marginal productivity is the additional unit of product obtained when an additional man-hour of labour is applied to the same land; and we can assert that surplus labour exists at the point where the value of the marginal product of labour is less than the subsistence requirement, or the rate of wages paid. The amount of surplus is measured by the excess of actual employment over the employment which equates marginal productivity and the subsistence requirement, or alternatively the wage rate.

The conflict which arises among our second, third, and fourth 'hand' of farming cultivator categories, however, is summed up in a statement by Norman (1968): 'As far as labour is concerned, it would appear realistic to expect male adults to work not much more than 5·0 hours a working day and a total of 1,200 hours or about 230 days a year.' And although we may postulate that the minimal amounts of work which an individual is prepared to undertake are determined by a number of factors many of which cannot readily be quantified, it is nonetheless useful to begin by examining the actual practice of two groups of farmers at the present time from the vantage point of estimates of marginal returns for additions of labour; for farm-family cultivators, even when operating at subsistence agriculture levels, seem to have a shrewd idea of when to stop applying labour as the analysis suggests, pointing to a fairly close correlation between theory and practice.

TABLE 7.1 *Productivity of resources in human and animal labour used in paddy production in two settlement areas of Mindanao, Southern Philippines 1970–71*

UPLAND PADDY			LOWLAND		
			kg/ha		
Gross product (geometric mean)	1,283		Gross product (geometric mean)		2,349
Human labour only					
Geometric mean inputs	*Average product*	*Marginal product*	*Geometric mean inputs*	*Average product*	*Marginal product*
hr/ha	*kg/hr paddy*	*kg/hr paddy*	*hr/ha*	*kg/hr paddy*	*kg/hr paddy*
369	3·47	1·17	428	5·48	1·76
Human plus animal labour					
526	2·44	0·50	686	3·42	0·87

SOURCE: Estimates based on data collected under the writer's supervision by staff of the Land Reform Council of the Philippines.

Theoretically, labour should be employed in each enterprise on the farm until its marginal value productivity in that enterprise equals the cost of the last unit of labour. In practice, farm-family labour was employed in these particular paddy enterprises, with large additions of hired labour which were paid in kind in paddy; cash payments for labour were exceptional.

The payments in kind made to labour offer a convenient and valid measure of how rationally the farmer is behaving. These averaged 1·202 kg/hr for upland paddy, and 2·117 kg/hr for lowland paddy; for human labour employed on upland paddy in particular, the wage rate can effectively be said to equal marginal productivity.

When this factor is looked at in the context of the farmers' relatively low yields, however, despite favourable climatic conditions and the abundant land resources of the region which are freely taken up if required without reference to any government agency, this suggests that cultivators may be deliberately optimising labour as the scarce resource.

Norman (1970) draws attention to the phenomenon of hired labour in a hand labour and low-income economy 'where funds are not readily available to pay for non-family labour'. He states that 'it could be hypothesised that the relative significance of non-family labour can be explained on the basis that most of it is hired during the bottleneck period'. This in fact was not supported in his case studies by an analysis of monthly man-hour inputs as percentages of total annual labour input on the family farm by family and non-family labour, which revealed very similar distributions. 'Logically,' Norman goes on 'one would expect a much larger percentage of total non-farm labour input to occur during the busiest period of the farming year.' He offers as a first possible explanation for his sample of three villages in Zaria Province of the North Central State of Nigeria the fact that 'a class of landless labourers has not yet arisen'.

Norman's results can be compared with farming practice in Gambia (Haswell, 1953), where adult males averaged a working day of only 5·7 hours, including time spent walking to and from their plots – a total of 627 hours in the year; excluding walking, the average time spent in the field was 5·1 hours a working day.

The total number of days worked by male adults on the family farm of 139 in Norman's study (weighted average for his three villages), is not so very different from the 110 in the Gambian sample. Unlike the Gambian example, however, female adult input is low for reasons which are institutional; in Gambia, female adults averaged 6·8 hours per working day, 6 hours excluding time spent walking to and from plots – a total of 155 working days over the year on the family farm, or 1,054 hours. Both these studies refer to an economy which relies entirely on hand labour for agricultural work which itself is confined to a short wet season of badly distributed rainfall.

Norman's study goes further, however, in measuring other occupations, which significantly increases the weighted average of days worked by adult males in his three villages from 139 to 226. The availability of non-farm occupations is to some extent determined by location; the analysis is particularly important, in that it divides these other occupations into those which are traditional consisting of those 'jobs that have been carried out for many generations', and those which have 'arisen directly or indirectly as a result of improved communications and the development of large cities, commercial firms, and governmental bodies'.

How far can van Dusseldorp's (1971) criteria be said to apply to Norman's villages? On a population basis (Norman, 1967), all fall into van Dusseldorp's classification: Additional primary centre with a 2 km radius of action.

TABLE 7.2   *Average number of days worked per adult male in three villages in Zaria Province, Nigeria: April 1966 to March 1967*

Village	Size of population	Location	Av. no. days worked by adult males			Per cent of days worked in non-farm occupations by adult males	
			Fam. farm	Other	Total	Traditional sector	Modern sector
Dan Mahawayim	663	Isolated*	140	123	263	96·3	3·7
Doka	1,025	40 km on main Kano– Zaria road	159	39	198	81·2	18·8
Hanwa	723	Urban Periphery					
Non-cattle owners			116	78	203	35·6	64·4
Cattle owners†			127	124	251	96·4‡	3·6

* 32 km from Zaria the last 11 km of which are motorable only during the dry season.
† In Hanwa, about 80 per cent of the Fulani families own cattle. Since these contribute significantly to their work responsibilities they have been separated from the predominantly Habe or Hausa families who own no cattle.
‡ Of which 84·3 per cent consists of looking after cattle.
SOURCES: Norman (1967, 1970).

Norman offers a commentary: 'The isolation of Dan Mahawayim has permitted it to continue in being fairly self sufficient and in preserving traditional crafts and services'; but he has classified trading as a traditional service, and it is important to note that 35 per cent of the 123 days' work in other occupations were spent in this manner.

Whereas Norman contrasts the isolated village with that of Hanwa in terms of traditional crafts which have largely been taken over by specialists in Zaria City, we can hypothesise that isolation, particularly in the absence of an all-weather road within a radius of action of both van Dusseldorp's additional primary centre and his primary centre if not in part his secondary centre also, leaves the way wide open for primary buyers to become not only the main buyers but also the isolated entrants to a market – a situation in which the individual buyer is often simply a communicative link, and, because of the isolated location, transportation costs incurred by farmers dispro-portionately high and the organisation of information to them poor.

Norman draws attention to the transfer of labour in other occupa-tions from the traditional to the modern sector which has occurred with increasing intensity in Doka and Hanwa, especially in Hanwa 'where the favourable location of the village has enabled workers to find jobs, usually of an unskilled nature, in the town'. He points, however, to an anomaly in Hanwa 'in that the cattle owners have confined themselves almost completely to looking after cattle and have not taken advantage of jobs available in the modern sector, although, of course, the city provides a large market for milk'; this is a factor which will be examined more closely in later discussion on the level of wages in non-farm occupations and the profitability of producing for the market protein-rich foods the demand for which rises with rising income. The position of Doka village Norman

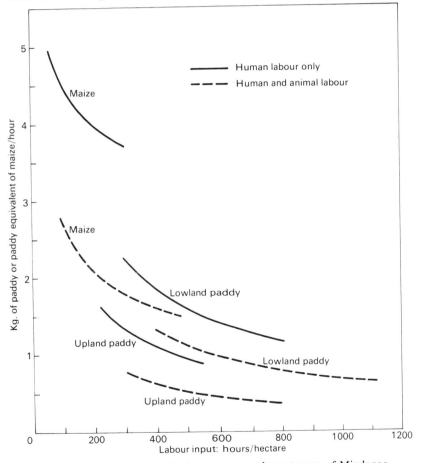

FIG. 2. Marginal productivity of labour: two settlement areas of Mindanao, Southern Philippines, 1970–71. (Farming practice: draught animals used for land preparation)

regards as unfortunate, 'not being sufficiently isolated to allow traditional craft and services to flourish in the absence of outside competition, while on the other hand, it is not sufficiently close to Zaria to provide off-farm employment opportunities for villagers'.

His attitude to trading as a subsidiary occupation – and he may be right under West African conditions, where there is a long history of petty trading – is that 'small-scale trading is an easy occupation to enter since it requires no technique or administrative skill and at this level very little capital'; of the total time spent in other occupations, that on trading fell from 35 per cent in Dan Mahawayim to 24·7 in Doka and only 3 per cent among the non-cattle owners in Hanwa. His general observation, which corresponds with that held by Bauer and Yamey (1961), is clearly valid, however, for that vast multitude of the tropical world which subsists by an economy in which cultivation is either entirely by hand or assisted by animal labour, that 'there is a rational tendency in developing countries for abundant labour being substituted for scarce capital in producing *tertiary* products thus inflating time devoted to such activities'.

Nevertheless we may question the continuing practice of an agriculture in which labour utilisation is at best no higher than 50 per cent even under conditions of multiple cropping, of which we have a classic example in one of the two settlement areas under study in Mindanao in Southern Philippines.

Table 7.1 compares the productivity of resources in human and animal labour used in upland and lowland paddy production; the region in which upland paddy is being grown, because season is not a scarce factor, is followed by a second crop, maize, in the same year. Triple-cropping of maize is possible and occasionally practised in Mindanao.

The geometric mean yield per hectare in the 1970–71 crop year was 1,283 kg for upland paddy and 992 kg for maize. Since the average practice secured a reward of 2·46 kg of maize per hour of additional (or marginal) labour per hectare compared with only 0·50 kg of paddy, we may question why farmers chose to grow upland paddy at all. Even when converted to paddy equivalents, the reward per hour devoted to maize is still greater. (The cost of hiring a work animal in the 1970–71 crop year was 0·69 kg/hr paddy equivalent.)

Von Oppenfeld *et al.* (1957) concluded from their study of farm management in the Philippines that some revision of cropping practices appeared to be indicated for the majority of paddy farmers, and recorded that maize was a profitable crop in Mindanao – returns to maize being highest compared with the rest of the country. They observed that the most common type of maize grown was White Flint, the favourite rice substitute in certain areas. Nevertheless, the von Oppenfeld study states that 'corn [maize], like upland palay [paddy], is a poor man's crop . . . Very possibly the upland palay farmer who is not too far from markets could make better use of his land by switching to more profitable enterprises such as orchard crops and vegetables. Only a few of the survey farms raised corn as a main enterprise.'

The preference for growing paddy over maize is perhaps a taste preference, rice being preferred to maize as food. Also rice stores better than de-husked maize; in the humid tropical Mindanao climate

TABLE 7.3   *Productivity of resources in human and animal labour used in upland paddy production followed by maize: Mindanao, Southern Philippines 1970-71*

Crop	Geometric mean inputs	Average product	Marginal product
		Human labour only	
	hr/ha	*kg/hr paddy*	*kg/hr paddy*
Upland paddy	369	3·47	1·17
		kg/hr maize	*kg/hr maize*
Maize	152	6·53	5·37
		kg/hr paddy equivalent	*kg/hr paddy* equivalent
		5·09	4·19
		Human plus animal labour	
Upland paddy	526	2·44	0·50
Maize	246	4·04	2·46 ⎞
		kg/hr paddy equivalent	
		3·15	1·92 ⎠

* Converted at prices paid in the local market.

in which rain falls throughout the year, with at most $1\frac{1}{2}$–3 dry months during which unusually weak winds contribute to the development of afternoon and evening thunderstorms, farmers probably have to de-husk maize to dry it adequately. Maize stored on the cob in one or two poor farm family households visited by the writer in Mindanao in 1971 was observed to be almost totally destroyed through excessive moisture.

Yet the average number of days worked over the year on all crop and livestock products by family-farm members is relatively low, and may be compared with observations made by Norman, despite the fact that, unlike Zaria Province in Nigeria, season is not a scarce factor.

A significant factor in this low labour utilisation economy is the relatively high number of days worked by certain age and sex groups in modern sector employment; this phenomenon has to be seen in conjunction with the fairly substantial hiring of labour both for upland paddy and for maize, some 31 per cent being hired for payment in kind in the former and 21 per cent in the latter crop.

The essential difference between the non-farm labour situation observed by Norman and that in Mindanao is that in the latter case, because of the use of water buffalo for land preparation, there is a shift from the general hiring of labour both within and outside peak periods of demand to concentration of hiring during the peak demand at harvest. This is to be expected where rice is grown which cannot

TABLE 7.4 *Average number of days worked by family members in a 'dry' farming settlement area of Mindanao 1970–71*

Status of worker	On-farm employment		Non-farm employment		Total
	All products	Care of work animals	Modern sector	Traditional sector	
Heads of households	109	30	5	70	214
Other adult* males	56	11	26	41	134
Adult females	21	10	41	35	107
Children†	30	6	Nil	9	45
			Labour utilisation under a‡ multiple cropping system		
			Heads of households	71·3	
			Other adult males	44·6	
			Adult females	35·6	
			Children	15·0	

* 15 years and over.
† 13 and 14 years; attending school.
‡ Based on a 300 working day year.

wait because of shedding and bird damage; maize can wait if there is not too much rain, but under Mindanao conditions of rainfall virtually throughout the year climate dictates the need for hastening the work of harvesting. Norman does in fact observe from his study in Zaria Province that 'the slight peak in farming activity in November is related to the harvesting of guineacorn'. In Zaria there is need for haste because of bird damage on sorghum.

The characteristic of hiring labour during off-peak periods of demand Norman suggests may be related to the high leisure preference particularly of heads of households, and here he identifies high leisure preference with 'a prestige element in being able to hire labour to work in the fields while the employer relaxes in the compound'. Indeed, it does appear from a number of economic studies that there is a failure to take account of the component: status, prestige, and power, as a primary factor in economic development; and that whereas it may take the form of high leisure preference in a traditional agriculture setting in which labour is available for hiring from within existing social institutions, younger men may look for money wages in non-traditional occupations not so much as a means of acquiring the necessities of life which are largely satisfied within the subsistence economy to which they have free access and which provides them with a sense of security, but for the consumption goods of a prestigious nature in the modern context of more affluent societies which can be bought with money wages.

This concept of money sought for conspicuous personal consumption, while a low labour input subsistence agriculture is starved of agricultural investment finance for increased production from agriculture, is a phenomenon which calls for an examination of patterns of consumption as a prerequisite to an understanding of production processes.

CHAPTER 8

The Incentive Effects of Consumption Privileges

*Income is a store of potential consumption, but it
also serves as a work incentive*

Lester C. Thurow (1971)

Even low-income communities at similar real income levels may have
widely different consumptions of food. A low-income elasticity of
demand for food nonetheless plays an important part in national
economic development.

What are the incentive effects that consumption privileges (income)
have on those individuals who seek employment in the non-farm
modern sector? Income elasticities are a reflection of the allocation of
income in the face of existing opportunities for expenditure; and the
income elasticity of demand – the proportional change in the quantity
of a good bought divided by the proportional change in income, price
remaining the same – is generally considered the best measure to use
when examining the consumption of goods such as food and clothing
which are consumed in substantial quantities at every level of income.

Rosauro (1961), however, in a study of households in rural Philippines, uses total consumption expenditures for income, and refers to
expenditure elasticity as the ratio of the relative increase (or decrease
when elasticity is negative) in expenditure on an item of consumption
to the corresponding relative increase in the total consumption
expenditures of the household.

He proceeds to define consumption of a consumer good as being
elastic if elasticity is found to be absolutely greater than one. Consumption is completely inelastic if elasticity is equal to zero; that is,
expenditure on an item is totally independent of increase or decrease
in the total consumption expenditures of the household. A negative
elasticity implies that a relative increase in the total consumption
expenditures is accompanied by a relative decrease in the consumption
of an item. Expenditure elasticities as an alternative to income
elasticities can be useful, Rosauro claims, in planning future demand

for consumer goods – although this method is not without defects. For example, if we are using a set of data of family expenditures at any given time to estimate income elasticity, we are liable to include, in both the highest and the lowest income groups, families who have only recently entered these groups, and have not yet adjusted their expenditure upwards or downwards to them.

In his analysis, Rosauro refers to inelasticity as being associated with necessity of consumption, and includes under this head food, fuel, light, and water as the basic necessities in the rural life of family households in the Philippines. 'Shelter and clothing appear to be barely elastic. On the other hand, education, recreation, transportation, personal care, and medical care may be considered as luxuries for the reason that consumption of each of these items is found to be highly elastic (elasticity is considerably greater than one)'.

TABLE 8.1 *Expenditure elasticities of consumption for rural households in the Philippines, 1957*

Food	0·872
Shelter	1·041
Fuel, light, water	0·807
Clothing	1·122
Tobacco	1·036
Transportation	1·568
Household operations	0·985
Personal care	1·373
Medical care	1·264
Recreation	1·526
Education	2·042

SOURCE: P. J. Rosauro (1961), p. 23; computed from PSSH data (March 1957 Survey).

Rosauro makes a particular point on concentration of expenditures:

As the level of income or total consumption expenditures continues to rise, the expenditure on an item with an increasing elasticity of consumption tends to rise at a rate much faster than the rate of income growth.

This suggests that the luxury items which are identified by high elasticities of consumption tend to be the monopoly of the higher-income group of households. That is, the distribution of expenditures on luxury items is generally concentrated among households in the higher-income level.

His attempt to demonstrate that disparity of distribution is closely associated with elasticity of consumption, and that expenditures on education, recreation, transportation, personal care, and medical care, which reveal the highest elasticities of consumption, appear to be concentrated among rural households of higher income levels, fails to disclose important patterns of behaviour among low-income farm-families who are subject to 'demonstration effect' – the desire to consume particular items by seeing them consumed by wealthy families in the neighbourhood. Many such expenditures arise out of borrowing, all too often at usurious rates of interest.

Goyoaga (1971), in a study of social differentiation in Ayutthaya the former capital of the kingdom of Thailand which lies 80 km north of Bangkok, found that 'education is one of the most important criteria for prestige ranking'. However, even from this point of view, the picture of a rather undifferentiated society still remains; only 3 per cent of this municipal town of approximately 40,000 people (of whom

17. Returning to the homestead from the paddy field at the end of the working day: Northeast Thailand.

18. Returning to the homestead from the maize (corn) field at the end of the working day: Mexico.

52 per cent of the population are under 20 years) had reached college level or its equivalent. A low correlation was found between

education and occupation, reflecting a blurred distinction between the unskilled workers, farmers, skilled workers and merchant groups. The relation between education and self-identification on a social scale is also low, while the relation between income and self-identification is higher, indicating that wealth is one of the best indicators of prestige ranking and social differentiation.

Goyoaga draws attention to the table which shows in terms of occupation that

farmers and sales account for almost two-thirds of the economically active population whereas, status-wise, self-employment and unpaid family work are the rule and not the exception. The manufacturing industry ranks fourth in Ayutthaya (17·8 per cent), but almost half (44 per cent) of this manufacturing industry consists of rice-mills and saw-mills.

In comparing productivity and income between farms in an economically advanced country, different products and costs are brought into account by expressing them all in money as a common unit.

Buck, however, working in China in the early 1930s, and at a later date de Vries in Indonesia, used grain equivalents as a more appropriate tool to measure output in a subsistence agriculture economy in which much of the produce consists of staple foodgrains and is home-consumed. In his studies of Asian countries, de Vries expressed all output in terms of *milled* rice per head of *total* population. Clark and Haswell (1970) draw attention to the fact that his method differed

19. Self-employed family members making lacquer-ware in Chiengmai.

20. Self-employed family member leaving his sacks of home prepared charcoal by the main highway in the hope of making a sale to a passing truck driver.

from that adopted by Buck who treated all grains equally, in that when dealing with a grain other than rice – millet for example, which has almost the same calorific value as milled rice but which sells at a lower price because it is much less palatable – he converted the particular grain into rice equivalents at prices prevailing in the local market.

It was when examining his own data that de Vries formulated his generalisation that the subsistence minimum in terms of kilograms of unmilled grain equivalent per person per year is a little under 300 kg – a figure which has been substantiated in a number of field studies, notably those of sociologists and anthropologists who reside for long periods in some of the more remote villages. As production

TABLE 8.2   *Economically active population by occupation*: Thailand (*percentages*)

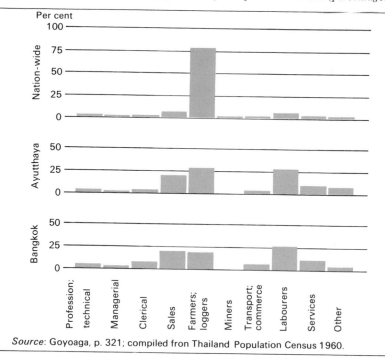

Source: Goyoaga, p. 321; compiled fron Thailand Population Census 1960.

rises, it is possible to sell some of the agricultural output in exchange for imports from a distance, or to employ a certain number of full-time craftsmen.

But below about 750 units, draught and meat animals alike have to live on straw, bran, and rough grazing; de Vries suggests that 600 units may be about the point at which communities find it possible to set aside some land for pasture. It is only beyond the productivity figure of about 750 units that there is enough grain to spare for regular feeding of livestock, particularly to pigs and poultry, who cannot digest cellulose as cattle do but require concentrated food in the form of grain or roots.

Drawing once more on Mindanao data as a test case in our enquiry, we again find that actual practice among low-income small-scale producers does not correspond in any precise way to theoretical concepts. With its relatively favourable climate and multiple cropping system, the use of draught animals, and the keeping of a few head of poultry and pigs, Tanaka's (1963) formula that when a farm household's marketing-ratio is above 80 per cent it can be said that it is producing for sale may be expected to apply; and indeed Table 8.3 in

TABLE 8.3   *Disbursement of receipts for consumption expenditures by a group of settlers on non-irrigated upland farms in Mindanao, Southern Philippines 1970–71*

Total receipts*	Farm products†			Marketing ratio	Proportion of total receipts from non-farm employment
	Retained	Sold	Tota		
	kg paddy equivalent/person/year			%	%
498	66	432	498	86·7	—
726	319	407	726	56·0	—

Below subsistence based on a consumption 'requirement' of 750 kg/person/year

952	214	738	952	77·5	—
1,039	266	773	1,039	74·4	—
1,082	233	849	1,082	78·4	—
1,143	399	744	1,143	65·0	—
1,269	474	485	959	50·5	24·4
1,285	323	962	1,285	74·8	—
1,906	288	1,618	1,906	84·8	—
1,952	600	1,352	1,952	69·2	—
2,040	274	1,766	2,040	86·5	—
2,234	367	1,054	1,421	74·1	36·4
2,438	422	1,203	1,625	74·0	33·3
2,857	135	1,401	1,536	91·2	50·9

* Including modern sector employment.
† Multiple cropping of upland paddy and maize for the supply of staple foodgrains; draught animals used for ploughing.

SOURCE: Data collected under the writer's supervision by staff of the Land Reform Council of the Philippines, a member of which Jose C. Macalindong, assisted with the analysis.

which marketing ratios do not even fall as low as 40 per cent, indicates that in no case can a farm-family household be said to be producing for home consumption as judged by Tanaka's criteria.

Clearly, employing Tanaka's indicator, farm family households appear to be market oriented. We have yet to examine supply responses in low-income agriculture; meanwhile, Tables 8.3 and 8.4 further call into question an assumption made by Rosauro that consumption expenditures on luxuries are concentrated among rural households of higher income levels. Even the poorest in the sample, whose total receipts in 1970 were well below subsistence 'requirement' – assuming the regular feeding of livestock – indulged in an expenditure on consumption luxuries as defined by Rosauro, which judged by the credit which that household obtained, constituted a relatively high proportion of total expenditure.

Tropical Farming Economics

TABLE 8.4 *Short-term borrowing for periods of six months or less by farm households in the settlement: Mindanao, Philippines, 1970–71*

| | Credit received from local moneylenders | | | | | | Annual rate of Interest | | |
| | Consumption expenditure | | | Production loan | Per cent of total loan | Debt repayment commitment as per cent of total receipts | Nec. | Lux. | Prod. loan |
Total receipts	Necessities	Luxuries	Total						
	Kg paddy equivalent/person/yr				%	%	%	%	%
498	27	113	140	71	33·6	42·4	106	60	60
726	92	92	184	69	27·3	34·8	120	120	120
Below subsistence based on a consumption 'requirement' of 750 kg/person/year									
952	26	—	26	39	6·0	6·8	100	—	90
1,039	110	—	110	—	0·0	10·6	120	—	—
1,082	250	61	311	171	35·5	44·5	120	60	60
1,143	—	—	—	—	—	—	—	—	—
1,269	—	319	319	—	0·0	25·1	—	60	—
1,285	39	—	39	—	0·0	3·0	120	—	—
1,906	204	—	204	241	54·1	23·3	36	—	24 48 } *
1,952	—	352	352	—	0·0	18·0	—	72	—
2,040	218	—	218	152	41·1	18·1	75	—	75
2,234	—	—	—	—	—	—	—	—	—
2,438	—	125	125	—	0·0	5·1	—	90	—
2,857	213	305	518	—	0·0	18·1	60	60	—

* 24 per cent interest rate for tractor hire; 48 per cent interest rate for purchase of a work animal. Necessities and luxuries are in accordance with Rosauro's classification; production loan includes credit for hire of tractor, purchase of draught animal, and the purchase of a plough.

What were these luxury consumption expenditures? As with the majority of the farm-family households, the main item of such expenditure was on education. Education, as Goyoaga found in Thailand, is one of the most important criteria for prestige ranking, and some family heads resorted to borrowing on a short-term basis from local moneylenders simply to meet this cost in respect of one or more of their children. Repayment is usually made in kind at the time of harvest, necessitating the sale of a substantial part of the harvest at a time when prices are low. It is significant that in the lower 'income' bracket interest rates on loans for necessities are 100 per cent and more; consumption expenditure under this head was mainly for staple foodgrains, and the harsher rates of interest reflect the lack of confidence among moneylenders in their clients' repaying capacity.

To treat medical care as a luxury item concentrated among rural households of higher income levels also overlooks an element of necessity in consumption expenditures; this may be illustrated by reference to one of the farm-family households under observation – that in which total receipts averaged 2,040 kg paddy equivalent per person in 1970 but in which a debt of 218 kg per person was nevertheless incurred in that year simply for food. 'This fellow is hardworking. From his farm income he has been able to buy and maintain a fairly good house; but in 1969 he got ill. He suffered from kidney trouble and he was bedridden for a period of three months. He spent all his savings for hospitalisation, and he was not able to work in his farm. He hired some farm labour from which he was able to produce a small amount for his family needs. He recovered from his illness and returned to work in 1970; with the help of hired labour and the hire of a tractor he was able fully to plant up his farm again, but during this period he was forced to borrow for food, and also to enable him to hire a tractor'.

A rather different case of borrowing for medicines as well as for food is that of the household whose total receipts averaged 1,082 kg per person in 1970; burdened by a debt repayment commitment as high as 44·5 per cent of his total receipts, this family head is suffering from tuberculosis 'and badly needs money for hospitalisation; he has resorted to gambling, and though part of the debt which he incurred was for the education of one of his children, he has not been able to continue to pay the fees and the child has been taken away from school'.

Haswell (1973) refers to the appalling neglect of the effects of sickness on tropical agriculture; for example, tuberculosis will be at a fully advanced stage at the peak of a man's economic activity, and when this strikes the head of a rural household there are serious economic effects caused by the loss of this man. To declare the problem requires a set of measurements from which it will be possible to correlate labour input with health status – a problem which is not simply a question of seasonal factors, but that the small man cannot afford to be sick while the bigger man can hire labour and get medical treatment.

Demands for *production* loans also exhibit certain distinctive characteristics: in one form or another they are all required for aids to human effort – the lightening of physical work, to replace a work animal, to acquire sufficient 'power' to deal with those operations where timeliness imposes a severe constraint; such loans have not been sought in this sample for modern industrial inputs like fertiliser or pesticides, though some use of the latter has been recorded.

Tables 8.3 and 8.4 strongly indicate the incentive effects that consumption privileges exert even to the 'release' from the family farm of some of its members who have been able to secure employment in the non-farm modern sector; Table 8.4 goes further to show the extent to which family households incur debt for consumption expenditures – not always to meet a personal catastrophe but on luxury items which they cannot afford.

A 'hidden' element in Rosauro's breakdown of consumption expenditures is the amount spent on dowries, weddings, and the like, which certainly under Asian conditions – might be almost more appropriately associated with necessity of consumption; for 'face' would be lost if custom were not strictly adhered to, and to lose face in a village is a fearful calamity. These constraints apart, the lure of consumer goods is still very tempting.

This brings into question the theory that farmers' choices will to a certain extent be conditioned by their evaluation of leisure relative to material possession – certainly as illustrated by the Mindanao sample of farms of upland paddy followed by a second crop, maize, in which a favourable climate minimises the problem of seasonal peaks of labour demand.

The work incentive of income is clearly apparent among heads of households whose labour utilisation averages some 71 per cent; but low levels of productivity caused by continued reliance on traditional agricultural practices, and the 'habit' of borrowing and the pledging of crops to meet certain consumption expenditures, invalidates this thesis without further enquiry into those factors which contribute to a state of affairs in which producers find themselves held in virtual bondage through striving after Thurow's 'consumption privileges'.

CHAPTER 9

The Trading Sector and the Volume of Marketing

*But in primitive rural communities in countries
where food is cheap in terms of prices of industrial
goods there appears to be little incentive to use
industrial inputs in agriculture*

Ester Boserup (1965)

Uma Lele (1971) attempts to evaluate the performance of the traditional trading sector in a study of foodgrain marketing in India. She recognises the paucity of research which has been done on the aggregate supply response to relative changes in sectoral prices, but states that 'the available evidence on the response of individual crops, of marketed surplus, and of input use suggests that though terms of trade may not, in themselves, be sufficient to bring about an agricultural revolution, they may accelerate or retard the growth rate initiated by a technological change'.

In seeking appropriate signals for substantial increases in agricultural production, she sets out to examine distributional processes, in particular the traditional market structure, the competitiveness of wholesale trade, the hypotheses that intermarket price differences do not tend to be greater than transport costs, that seasonal fluctuations in prices are consistent with storage costs, and that milling margins are commensurate with milling costs and milling out-turns.

It is the volume of marketing, and the seasonality of marketing, by producers in the second, third, and fourth 'hand' of farming that immediately calls our attention, however, in an attempt to provide some assessment of private sector practices in trading, and their consequences.

In a statement on rice marketing in the Philippines, the Board of Administrators of the Rice and Corn Administration (1968) report that 'some of the bleak features of our agricultural economy are the low level of education and chronic indebtedness of the farmers, low yields per unit of land, primitive methods of agriculture, and defective marketing system. The marketing system is disorderly and trader-controlled. This is particularly so in grain marketing.' This statement introduces their programme for the procurement of paddy sufficient to support paddy prices and to accumulate a buffer stock aimed at price stabilisation and to meet unexpected shortages; but it is not without some justification that the RCA has been by some renamed 'Return to Camote Again'. Camote, the sweet potato, is the poor man's food, and, despite the highminded aims set out in their programme, for the producer the situation remains essentially unchanged.

It is a well-known fact anywhere in the tropics that opinion has it that traders batten on farmers; but it is the traders who provide a service in the disposal of produce. Without traders the farmers would be helpless; an acceptable alternative has yet to be found by any state service. Meanwhile the risks are borne by the traders, who must profit to live; and it is they who come to the rescue of the farmer in an emergency – for example, if a child is sick – and not government help which, though excellent in theory, calls for much paper work and delay. The trader is prompter, and often more sympathetic, even if expensive.

For relatively undeveloped Mindanao, the evidence confirms the RCA's report that 'past experience shows that prices of [paddy] in major producing areas fluctuate to as much as 30 to 40 per cent between the main harvest and the lean months period'; what is more disturbing, however, is that not only has the situation remained unchanged in many areas since the inception of the RCA, in others it has worsened – notably in areas of political insecurity.

Can the agricultural sector tolerate government interference? Does not Uma Lele herself stop short her own investigations at the very point of departure from the normal operation of market forces when examining private sector performance?

We may begin by examining actual practice in grain movements off-farm which is distinctly different from stating the case in terms of marketing ratio or marketable surplus. But marketing ratio is not an altogether irrelevant measure. For example, while recognising the scanty existence and generally poor quality of data, Uma Lele thereby avoids a thorough analysis of farm prices, though she briefly quotes a Government *Report on the Pace and Pattern of Market Arrivals* – with particular reference to the restriction on export of paddy and rice from the surplus districts in 1957, 1958, and 1959, such as Burdwan and Birbhum districts of West Bengal.

She draws attention to the fact that in 1958 and 1959 ceiling prices of paddy and rice were fixed by the Government, which, in West Bengal, resulted in farm prices which were lower than market prices in 1958, whereas in 1959 they were higher. She postulates that

the higher farm-level prices in 1959 may have been due to the increased tendency of millers to purchase in the villages to avoid controls at the market level. As 1959 was the second successive poor crop year in West

Bengal, the pressure on supplies had increased and had to be reflected in higher farm prices.

In 1959 the farm harvest prices for Burdwan and Birbhum districts showed greater disparity than in any other year for which data were examined. This seems to have been a result of inter-district movement restrictions, which created varying supply imbalances in the two surplus regions.

The bypassing of official restrictions by millers through purchasing direct in the villages assumes good access roads; and indeed Uma Lele does point out that 'the Grand Trunk Road, a major National highway, passes through Burdwan'. However, the phenomenon of a price difference greater than transport costs appeared to exist in Birbhum district which she states was at a disadvantage because it was poorly connected by roads to neighbouring areas.

Nor can the study of foodgrain marketing in low-productivity low-income sectors as are typified in the second, third, and fourth 'hand' of farming be divorced from that of the study of consumption expenditure, and ability to store in the expectation of price increases, among farm family households; in other words, so complex are the factors at the 'farm level' which influence the marketing of foodgrains that it may well be misleading to attempt to explain year-to-year variations in the seasonal price pattern as being determined by changes in production and/or arrivals from harvest until the off-seasonal peak.

'The palay [paddy] is already in the city during lean time or period of off-season', the Mindanao small-scale farmer complains. And the evidence is that it might as well be in the city if the farmer has to buy back from the village trader at off-seasonal peaks. The retail or final price paid by the ultimate consumer is a measure of the welfare of farmers as consumers. Table 9.1 shows the difference between the average price received by primary wholesale handlers and the average price received by retail food stores in a given period, and indicates the retailers' gross margin although the cost of milling and other services such as secondary wholesaling and cartage are normally present.

Because of the long hauls of paddy between village and city – an upper limit of 135 km employing heavy motor trucks – indications are that primary wholesalers' gross margins are not greater than transport costs which, for long hauls, average about 31 per cent of the gross value of the product – a high cost which does not warrant the transportation of a low-value product over long distances.

The hidden gains or speculative profits, however, belong to the village trader who sells back to the producer at off-seasonal peaks at, from observation, an average price which corresponds closely to that paid by the ultimate consumer in the city; from this, it can be

TABLE 9.1   *Producer's share of final product in the marketing of paddy and vegetables*

	Price index*	Gross margin
I. Paddy		
Final price to consumer in city as milled rice purchasing from retailer	100·0	
City retailer's margin		26·0
Wholesaler in primary market trucking between village and city	74·0	
Wholesaler's margin		12·0
Village trader purchasing from producer at 'farm-gate' within an 8 km radius of village	62·0	
Trader's margin		24·0
Producer price	38·0	
II. Vegetables		
Final price to consumer in city purchasing from retailer	100·0	
City retailer's margin		17·2
Retailer purchasing from city wholesaler	82·8	
City wholesaler's margin		15·4
City wholesaler purchasing from local merchant trucking from 'buying point'	67·4	
Local merchant's margin		54·9
Producer price at 'buying point' on highway	12·5	

* Final price (April 1970 base) = 100.

TABLE 9.2   *Off-seasonal peaks in foodgrain* prices at village trader level (percentage increase over harvest price)*

Crop year	Paddy†	Maize‡	Off-seasonal price of maize relative to paddy
1966/7	54·5		0·50
1967		13·0	
1967/8	37·0		0·75
1968		75·0	
1968/9	0·0§		
1969		100·0	
1969/70	63·0		0·58
1970		161·0	

* Multiple cropping of paddy followed by maize.
† From July to May.
‡ From November to May.
§ No marketable surplus.

inferred that the village trader is in full possession of market intelligence even though the city is many kilometres away from the producing area; and indeed, the RCA (1968) have drawn attention to what they call the 'buy-store and mill later' trade scheme in which the speculative profits of the village trader have run to as high as 50 per cent of the selling price of rice.

Uma Lele (1971) makes an assessment of storage costs of paddy and rice in Tamil Nadu and West Bengal. 'The interviews with the traders in the two States indicated that, contrary to the general impression that storage losses are heavy, they seem fairly low, at least in the trading sector'; and in her analysis she assumes an average loss in weight due to drying of 4 per cent and an average loss due to pests and insects of 1·25 per cent in a period of eight months – although she points out that in a personal exchange of views with Dorris Brown he rejected such low estimates of loss in weight on the basis of his observations in Tamil Nadu (Brown, 1971) 'and argues in favour of a range of 2 per cent to 10 per cent'. Traders can reduce storage losses caused other than by dryage, but to do so costs money for insecticides; and they have been known to say that 'it is cheaper to suffer the loss'.

In that the village trader's gross margin as indicated in Table 9.1 (24 per cent) is considered relatively high when purchasing from the producer, this is largely a reflection of the high initial costs of transport from farm gate to village because of poor offline road conditions; at greater distances than an 8 km radius from the village, wherever road conditions were found to be so bad as to be almost impassable, producers' share was observed to fall from 38 per cent to 16 per cent. During 1970 this region of Mindanao also suffered political disturbances and heightened insecurity, further affecting producers' share of final product in the marketing of paddy which fell to the negligible figure of 9 per cent.

Maize, the alternative cereal grown under a multiple cropping system, is not the preferred food grain, and prices do not fluctuate widely excepting when there is no marketable surplus of rice as in 1968–69. All producers would like to grow some paddy, and only if they are particularly short of labour will they confine themselves to double-cropping maize instead because it is less labour-demanding.

This is not to say that the decision to grow paddy in this region is necessarily right in economic terms. In fact, it may even be viewed as a 'social cost' in the sense that it results in a misallocation of resources in labour as measured by output per worker, and leads to a 'hungry season gap' which affects welfare; for, although it would appear that primary wholesalers' gross margins may roughly be equated with transport costs, it is the extent to which producers make use of local buyers which indicates the degree of indebtedness for subsistence needs, and this in turn is a reflection of low output per unit of area.

Dimacutac and Escalante, in a study of farm prices of selected products, reveal the proportion of paddy in three areas of Bukidnon Province in Mindanao which, in 1963–64, were handled by the local store – which suggests favourable terms of trade for consumer goods:

Local store 62·89 per cent; *Village middlemen*, 37·11 per cent.

In a similar study by Cabrera in 1960, local buyers were considered the most important as sources of credit, and 78 per cent of his sample in fact borrowed for food and 'other personal needs'. He also refers to the choice of outlet or buyer by the farmer as being dictated by the ability to obtain credit during the off-harvest season. Merchants use this opportunity to supply credit as a means of encouraging farmers to place their business with them, and add their margin to the price of the supplies sold to the farmer.

We may tentatively conclude from these studies that the consumer goods available in local stores for which producers have not the means to procure but are encouraged to purchase by local store-owners, has adverse effects the cost of which does not fall on the local buyers. In this sense, enslavement in a perpetual round of debt eventually becomes a cost to society in terms of production foregone through persistent poverty, and consequential inefficiency and ill-health.

The argument that local sources of credit carry high interest rates because loans are usually made without security may be questioned, for the evidence is that almost without exception these are short-term loans repayable at harvest; Dimacutac and Escalante bring another important factor into their study, that of the high proportion of paddy which is sold off the field at the point of harvest which, for some varieties, was 100 per cent in their sample. In other words, local buyers who had made loans collected debts plus interest in paddy immediately it was reaped before the harvested crop could be transported back to the farmstead, or local market, and sold else-where.

Anne Martin (1963) gives comparative figures for prices realised by producers in Uganda selling retail in the local markets and those obtainable by sale to local merchants, and stresses the importance of direct sales in the local markets by growers. 'It is often by far the most profitable way to dispose of small quantities, precisely because the local market is a very narrow one, dealing in small total quantities in very small units of sale.'

But of finger millet, Martin states that in some areas it

is the first saleable product after the 'hungry gap', and farmers tend to sell it then at a low price, buying it back later with the proceeds of the cotton crop. Not surprisingly, in these conditions, its domestic price is observed to fluctuate directly with the returns from cotton. . . . It is pre-eminently a crop worth holding, a profit of 50 per cent being often obtainable by selling after four or five months, and its storage qualities are in fact excellent (p. 6).

TABLE 9.3   *Local merchants' gross margin*

Crop	Margin*
Mixed beans	50
Sesame	1–25
Cowpeas	50
Groundnuts (shelled)	44–50
Finger millet	0–20

* Final price for products retailed in Lira, local market (September 1961) = 100
SOURCE: Martin, (1963) p. 18.

In Mountain Province in the far North of the Philippines climatic conditions are suitable for temperate crops, and vegetable producers predominate over much of the area; but transport rates for the 'journey to mountainsides' by contractors trucking vegetables are high wherever roads are bad and the risk of landslides severe. Contractors pick up from roadside buying points; there is a further transport cost which cannot be ignored, that of carrying vegetables on the shoulder up and down steep slopes to the roadside.

Producers in the vicinity of Baguio City were digging in their vegetables in the latter half of 1968 whenever the price fell to a low of 3 centavos per kilogram; at that price the cost of transporting vegetables to Manila, the market outlet and a distance of 257 km, was as high as 83 per cent of the gross value of the crop (Haswell, 1970).

Observations made in 1970 in southern Philippines summarised in Table 9.1 indicate that, assuming it is profitable to produce the particular vegetable and given positive economic response, if transport costs are to be kept below one-third of the gross value of the product, as they should be, then transport by head or shoulder from 'farm gate' to buying point cannot exceed a distance of from 0·5 to 1 km because of the extremely high cost of transport by this method; at greater distances, it becomes cheaper for large cities to fly in fresh vegetables produced commercially to high standards of quality and packing.

Local merchants, who are seen in Table 9.1 to gain the highest proportion of final price, carry the main burden of risk, particularly if motor vehicles break down on long hauls because of bad road surfaces and delivery is delayed, since deterioration is rapid.

In practice, most merchants have to diversify their operations because of the seasonality of production of a single vegetable. A further hazard is that the merchant may not obtain a quick sale when he reaches the city, with consequent high wastage rates due to the perishable nature of the product – unless processing and canning industries, which are nevertheless additional costs in production for final consumption, exist.

In this sense, food crops marketed by small-scale producers in the second, third, and fourth 'hand' of farming, wherever long hauls are involved are 'cheap' at the farm gate and 'dear' by the time they are available for final consumption; and we may question what are the economic incentives which rural communities really have to use industrial inputs in agriculture.

CHAPTER 10

Industrial Inputs: Adoption and Performance

Producing more per hectare and per man is the
best way to reconcile the apparent conflict between
output and welfare goals

Lehman B. Fletcher *et al.* (1970)

'There are two sides to agricultural marketing. One side includes those activities connected with the movement, handlings, storage, processing and distribution of food commodities from the time they leave the farm until they reach the final consumer. The other involves the movement of agricultural inputs from the manufacturer to the farmer'; and the authors of *Guatemala's Economic Development: the Role of Agriculture* (Fletcher *et al.*) continue with the observation that 'the markets for inputs and outputs are closely related'.

But are they?

For the rural sector, the transport element in the cost of industrial goods, because of the generally poor communications systems which prevail, prices many inputs right off the market; alternatively, the decision to apply an industrial input, for which a price has to be paid in cash, may be at a level significantly below that required for optimum results.

The use of fertilisers and insecticides takes us into the fifth 'hand' of farming; and we shall first examine the hypothesis that these industrial inputs are not generally applied unless or until the fourth 'hand' of farming – the use of water requiring a network of dykes and ditches – has been established.

Takase and Kanō (1969) summarise the process of development by reference to stages of development of rice yields; regions which fall within the lower limits suffer, in their analysis, from a serious lag in water resource development. They record the following figures (p. 529):

	tons/ha
Natural conditions (1952)	0·6–1·5
Flood irrigation (1957)	2·0
Ditch and Dyke irrigation (1962)	2·5
Fertiliser application with irrigation (1965)	3·3–3·6

The yield data shown in Table 10·1 for a settlement area in which producers are growing paddy under natural conditions, clearly illustrate Takase and Kanō's thesis. However, although this group falls within the third 'hand' of farming – employing draft animals – farm households in the upper income stream did use insecticides, which, theoretically, belongs to a later stage of development.

Sandoval, Hsieh, and Gaon (1967) in a study of 769 farmers in Plaridel, approximately 42 km north of Manila, point out that

> proper irrigation and judicious use of fertiliser, insecticide, and weedicide helps maximise yield. This has been clearly proved on the experimental level, but it is not yet known whether use of these items of inputs can perform as profitably on the farm level . . . no differences in production are apparent in the use of fertiliser, insecticide and weedicide either singly or in combination. However, farmers using insecticide achieved a slightly higher yield than any of the other combinations.

TABLE 10.1   *The relationship between production and use of industrial inputs:* *non-irrigated upland paddy in a settlement area of Mindanao remote from a large urban centre, 1970–71*

Total receipts	Production expenditure			Production loan	Yield	Proportion of total receipts from non-farm employment
	Fertiliser	Insecticides	Weedicides			
person/ year	kg paddy equivalent ha	ha	ha	ha	tons/ ha	%
498	—	—	—	71	1·7	0·0
726	—	—	—	23	1·3	0·0

Below subsistence based on a consumption 'requirement' of 750 kg/person/year

952	—	—	—	20	1·0	0·0
1,039	—	—	—	—	1·3	0·0
1,082	—	—	—	171	1·2	0·0
1,143	—	—	—	—	1·2	0·0
1,269	—	29	—	—	1·2	24·4
1,285	—	—	—	—	1·1	0·0
1,906	—	—	—	80	1·1	0·0
1,952	—	24	—	—	0·9	0·0
2,040	—	—	—	152	1·6	0·0
2,234	—	18	—	—	1·3	36·4
2,438	—	10	—	—	1·1	33·3
2,857	—	76	—	—	1·9	50·9

* Converted at prices paid in the local market.

The yield effect in the five cases where farmers reported using insecticide in the Mindanao study of upland paddy producers appears to be nil: it is of some significance, however, that although production loans were sought by producers with widely ranging incomes, those who used insecticides were not only in the higher income group but did not seek loans for production. On the contrary, in four of the five cases, a substantial income was derived from non-farm sources.

Table 10.2 points to an almost universal use of insecticides on irrigated paddy in income groups above the subsistence 'requirement' of 750 kg paddy equivalent per person per year, as defined for a

TABLE 10.2 *The relationship between production and use of industrial inputs: irrigated paddy in a settlement area of Mindanao accessible to a large urban centre, 1970–71.*

Total receipts	Production expenditure				Production loan	Yield	Proportion of total receipts from non-farm employment
	Ferti-liser	Insecti-cides	Fungi-cides	Weedi-cides			
person/ year	kg paddy equivalent ha	ha	ha	ha	ha	tons/ ha	%
136*	—	—	—	—	—	2·9*	0·0
596	—	—	—	—	—	1·7	17·3
732	—	—	—	—	—	2·4	0·0

Below subsistence based on a consumption 'requirement' of 750 kg/person/year

755	—	63	—	—	—	2·3	0·0
869	58	14	—	30	—	2·1	0·0
1,110	—	50	—	—	—	2·6	0·0
1,679	—	16	—	10	2,222	2·9	54·4
1,813	—	12	—	—	—	2·6	0·0
2,046	—	—	—	—	—	2·5	36·6
2,228	—	3	—	—	—	1·5	0·0
2,316	—	13	—	—	—	2·4	35·1
2,343	—	17	—	52	266	2·7	0·0
2,410	—	16	—	—	—	2·1	0·0
2,434	—	31	31	—	—	2·5	59·5
2,445	—	31	—	—	—	2·8	64·9
4,129	—	27	14	—	—	2·0	29·1
6,138	—	—	—	—	—	2·4	0·0

* Tenant with only 0·25 ha paddy land and a large family of eleven in the household.

SOURCE: Data collected under the writer's supervision by staff of the Land Reform Council of the Philippines, a member of which, Jose C. Macalindong, assisted with the analysis.

community employing draft animals on the assumption that regular feeding of livestock is practised. This settlement has access to ditch and dyke irrigation (made available by cooperative effort between the settlers and the government at relatively low capital cost); and some 50 per cent of producers in the sample do appear to fall within Takase and Kanō's classification of ditch and dyke irrigation on the basis of output.

There is no real evidence that the higher yields obtained in this settlement compared with that of the upland paddy producers are more than a function of water resource development, despite the 'regular' use of insecticides and, in one or two cases, also of weedicides. Of greater significance is the effect of ditch and dyke irrigation on income levels with some examples of producers who neither sought loans for the purchase of industrial inputs nor employment outside farming as security to meet basic consumer needs; for the availability of water reduces dependence on uncertain rainfall. 'It is rare for the seasonal pattern of precipitation to coincide with crop water requirements and often, even in humid areas, short-term deficiencies in soil moisture can occur which check crop growth and reduce financial returns', Carruthers (1968) reminds us, but goes on to warn from his Pakistan experience that 'in irrigation project planning there is often bias towards engineering aspects of design and consequent neglect of agricultural considerations without realisation that the reasons for investment are to stimulate agriculture'.

How can farmers economise with scarce peak supplies? He offers the following suggestions:

1. by changing cropping patterns;
2. by efficiency in distribution and application;
3. by allowing crops to draw upon stored soil moisture;
4. by allowing low value crops to suffer water stress;
5. by fulfilling leaching requirement at other times;
6. by using economic rather than technical criteria for determining application.

The most direct measure of the economic value of irrigation water is whether farmers purchase and sell freely among themselves. In Mysore State in India, owners of small electrically operated irrigation pumpsets in a 'dry' area were observed selling water at a fixed price per irrigation, regardless of the type of crop grown. Crop-wise, charges for supplying water for rice reached almost one ton paddy equivalent per hectare, but only half this amount for tobacco, dropping to one-sixth for tobacco grown during the rains and requiring several less irrigations; the charge for sorghum, a drought resistant crop, was minimal (Haswell, 1967).

The effects of persistent watering to excess can create serious problems of waterlogging and soil salinisation; and, in part to exert some control in the use of water provided by public investment, in part because of the additional income generated by the provision of irrigation facilities, recipients should bear some charge. Water rates should bear a relationship to the crop grown and the amount of water consumed. But at this very point of water resource development we find in practice more evidence of stationariness in agricultural production than in other stages of development.

Criticism has been levelled at the public sector policy of undercharging for irrigation water in the Philippines; a flat rate charge of 12·50 pesos per hectare per year was applied before 1965 for schemes financed by World Bank loans; but the constantly worsening debt position led in that year to an increase in the water rate to 60 pesos per hectare per year for rice on the basis of 25 pesos for the wet season crop and 35 pesos for the dry season crop. In effect, water is just provided by the public sector, and its application is not measured; and so even at this higher charge the government has found itself still heavily subsidizing the supply of irrigation water to the farmer.

Meanwhile, the demand for privately purchased water pumpsets has escalated, and farmers without pumps are purchasing water from

21. Volunteers among the local farmers damming a stream for ditch and dyke irrigation in a Mindanao settlement.

those who have pumps for which they are prepared to pay a water charge of 160 pesos per hectare per crop (320 pesos per hectare per year) – or, in terms of paddy at market prices prevailing in the rice bowl region of Central Luzon during the writer's visit in 1971, equivalent to about 0·25 m ton per crop and about 0·5 m ton per year for areas which are double-cropped.

22. Weeding paddy crop grown in the settlement following ditch and dyke irrigation in Mindanao.

Ishikawa (1967) defines categories of inputs contributing most to output increase as leading inputs, and gives high priority to irrigation and fertiliser; for 'even in Asia, where the dominant patterns of agriculture are influenced by the monsoon, there are areas in some countries which belong to really dry regions like the Near East. In these areas, the effect of irrigation upon land productivity is similar to that in the Near East.'

But he makes the important point that

even though irrigation ratios are similar between two areas, the productivity effects of irrigation are quite different because of the difference of the technical qualities of irrigation facilities. . . . In many countries of Asia, irrigation means simply the making up for insufficient rainfall by a simple device without adequate facilities of storing, field-channelling and drainage . . . in most countries in South and South-east Asia where land productivity is very low, marginal increases in productivity seem to be most significantly explained by the irrigation ratio. . . . Irrigation may be said to be the leading input in such a productivity stage.

One of Ishikawa's most important contributions, however, is the line of demarcation which he draws beyond this point which he classifies as

23. Successful farmer in Southern Thailand: he has diversified crop production and introduced livestock enterprises.

the first role of irrigation, in that its main function is that of stabilising the harvest fluctuations due to deficient or untimely rainfall.

It is when irrigation makes possible the introduction of a second crop, and when it makes possible increased application of fertiliser, the use of improved seeds, and farming techiques, that 'the quality of the existing irrigation facilities must often be improved. . . . Among

24. Large-scale irrigation project in the dry zone of Sri Lanka showing inadequate field-channelling and drainage resulting in poor distribution of water to producers' paddy plots.

these inputs (other than irrigation), there seem to be some complementarity relation in which any one of these inputs cannot be increased effectively without being accompanied by an increase in others.' This is the stage when the explanatory strength of irrigation is receding; and the real issue to be faced is that the adoption of some cultural practices as shown in Table 10.2 is associated with a level of irrigation which simply makes up for insufficient rainfall.

The mere application of industrial inputs by producers in these circumstances has not led to a shift in crop cultivation from one input-output combination to another with a higher productivity, and it cannot therefore be said that the fifth 'hand' of farming has yet been reached; for the whole of the increase in output as between the non-irrigated upland paddy and the irrigated lowland paddy shown in Tables 10.1 and 10.2 is explained by irrigation facilities of a rudimentary kind. It is seldom effective applying an input unless that input is a limiting factor. If water is the limiting factor then until that is put right other inputs such as fertiliser do not pay. Similarly, it is a waste to spray insecticide on a poor crop, say cotton, because it will give only a small return.

Labour, the role of additional labour input, is not considered as a 'leading input' by Ishikawa who, nonetheless, recognises that in the vast peasant sectors of the contemporary developing countries in Asia the contribution of total labour to total agricultural output seems dominant; yet we can hypothesise that total employment, and the structure of the farm labour force including the factors which determine the magnitude of the working days for non-agricultural production, directly influences farmers' behaviour at all levels of agricultural production activity in early stages of economic development, and takes precedence over prospects for substantial increases in land productivity by an increased application of industrial inputs.

CHAPTER 11

The 'So-called' Need for Higher Education

Despite great differences in climate, technology, and output mix, it seems apparent that the major variations in land and labour productivity among countries are associated with differences in the levels of industrial inputs which ease constraints imposed by the inelastic supply of the primary factors

Yujiro Hayami and Vernon W. Ruttan (1971)

Schultz (1964) concludes, with respect to the doctrine that a part of the labour working in agriculture in poor countries has a marginal productivity of zero, that this is a false doctrine. In *Transforming Traditional Agriculture* he states as evidence for arriving at this conclusion that 'it fails to win any support when put to a critical test in analysing the effects upon agricultural production of the deaths in the agricultural labour force caused by the influenza epidemic of 1918–19 in India'. He points out that 'in general, the provinces of India with the highest death rates attributed to the epidemic also had the largest percentage declines in acreage sown to crops', and presents data which shows, for all British India at that time, a predicted decrease in agricultural production of 3·3 per cent and an observed reduction in acreage sown of 3·8 per cent attributed to deaths resulting from the influenza epidemic.

The later work of Luning (1969) states this doctrine more explicitly as a working hypothesis: 'Agricultural wages in these low income peasant economies reflect labour's marginal productivity value to the employer. Moreover, the marginal productivity of family labour in farming is not zero'; and he identifies unemployment in rural areas as being partly the result of lack of incentives in the economic system and partly caused by excess of the aggregate labour supply in relation to the supplies of cooperating inputs. This hypothesis fails to take account of the participation or activity rate, which can vary widely from region to region within countries, being dependent primarily on the age structure of the population, the degree of female participation, and production foregone in terms of those members of the population in educational institutions who would otherwise constitute additions to the labour force.

There is every indication that even the poorest peasant producer places a high value on education; and this value is reflected in the excessive debt burden which such farm-family households undertake. What we may question is whether the type of education available will yield a stream of extra earnings which justify the costs in terms of earnings foregone during education.

Furthermore, the private costs incurred in obtaining education cannot be seen solely as earnings foregone by the individual during education, but as net income foregone by farm family households through reduction of the family labour force, and the consequential increase in the dependancy ratio; that education is not an investment but a consumption in these circumstances is apparent from the persistence of producers practising a low productivity traditional agriculture. which they deprive almost entirely of investment funds, and, among those of their number who have passed through all levels of schooling, their almost universal failure to serve that sector of society from which they have originated. This latter situation is in part caused by the types of educational institutions available, the majority of which lead to clerical and government job expectations. When these are not realised school-leavers and college graduates (especially in the arts) swell the ranks of the unemployed and further congest urban cities rather than take up the alternative of returning to work on the family farm.

Table 11.1 illustrates the value placed on education in our southern Philippines' sample of farm-family households of upland paddy and maize producers. In general, education is dominated by private enterprise, although primary schools in remote and poor areas are served by local *municipios.*

Participation rates in the labour force on the family farm exclude children of primary school age; all other age groups have an economic value as workers, and the productivity foregone where farm family heads of households have released some of their number for higher education is a factor which places additional labour high in the list of priorities of leading inputs; in part, earnings foregone (net income to family labour) can be measured from payments made to additional non-family labour or labour substitutes; in part, indebtedness for education constitutes a measure of industrial inputs foregone of which fertiliser is probably the most important for increased output per unit of area.

A distinction should be made between irrigated and non-irrigated areas in our sample, with particular reference to the additional advantages of the irrigated area of relatively good road networks and

TABLE 11.1 *Expenditure on education and levels of indebtedness for education in a relatively remote Mindanao settlement area 1970–71*

Size of family		Total receipts from farm and non-farm activities	Fees and maintenance costs of educational institutions attended by some school-age members of farm households	Proportion of total receipts if paid in full by farm household	Loans secured in 1970 (plus interest charges) for educational purposes	Proportion of total receipts (excluding loan) if paid in full by farm household
No.	Of whom in full-time non-farm employment					
		At 1970 price tags of a year of schooling* kg. paddy equivalent/person/year/farm household				
5	0	1,082	—	—	—	—
6	0	1,285	21	1·6	—	—
7	0	2,040	53	2·6	—	—
4	0	1,039	47	4·5	—	—
11	0	1,906	154	8·1	—	—
9	0	2,234	341	15·2	—	—
9	1	952	188	19·7	—	—
8	0	726	55†	7·6	92†	†
13	0	498	276	55·4	113	32·7
10	2	2,857	307	10·7	305	Negligible

Farm households with one member receiving college education and required to live away from home

10	0	1,143	912	79·8	—	—
9	1	2,438	875	35·9	125	30·8
11	0	1,269	858	67·6	319	42·5
9	0	1,952	910	46·6	352	28·6

* Primary 125, elementary 188, High School 1,190, College 7,561 kg paddy equivalent.
† Actual amount of loan 61 kg paddy equivalent/person/year/farm household; high interest rate charged.

accessibility to an urban area. This is reflected in the higher proportion of family members in full-time non-farm occupations, and the higher proportion of family members in high school.

Examination of those households in receipt of earnings from non-farm occupations reveals that, by their very nature, they add nothing to production; on the contrary, in some cases they are decidedly exploitive.

One of the households recorded in Table 11.1, with ten family members (two of whom are employed in non-farm occupations) and a total income greater than any other household in the sample, derived a considerable proportion of its income from loaning paddy to other households during the lean period of the year, repayable at harvest at interest rates of 100 per cent and over; the two members in full-time non-farm employment are daughters one of whom is a school teacher and the other a municipal clerk in a municipality containing a population of 16,577 according to the 1970 population census of the Philippines (Anon, 1971). In fact this household, as Table 11.1 illustrates, obtained an educational loan of 305 kg paddy equivalent from a business associate which was repaid in kind after the maize harvest, although it would appear that in their 'financial' circumstances it was not necessary to seek a loan. The solution to the enigma lies in the opportunity to borrow 'at no interest' from co-partners in business, without having to dip into the product from their own holding which is securing for them very high rates of interest through the practice of loaning food grains to poorer families to meet seasonal shortages.

In examining education for consumption, Schultz (1971) states the case for the three components: education for current consumption, education for longer period future consumption (making it an investment in an enduring consumer component), and education for skills and knowledge useful in economic endeavour and thus an investment in future earnings.

In only one instance in our sample has education resulted in skills which have led to future earnings, that of a mechanic in a pineapple plantation. In a sense, however, this has not added to the local stock of education as the acquisition of a skill led to out-migration; Table 11.2 reinforces this problem for the small-scale producer which shows

TABLE 11.2   *Comparative educational advantages and the consequential effects on the dependancy ratio of urban-orientated farm family households 1970–71*

Educational institution	Irrigated and accessible to sizeable urban area	Non-irrigated and remote from sizeable urban area
	Population in educational institution	
	%	%
Primary	10·56	13·58
Elementary	13·00	17·90
High school	13·82	8·64
College	3·25	3·70
	40·63	43·82
Labour force as per cent of total population		
Farm	17·07	32·71
Non-farm	7·31	4·32
	24·38	37·03
Dependancy ratio:		
per farm worker	4·43 : 1	1·90 : 1
per worker	3·10 : 1	1·68 : 1

the high proportion of young persons moving up the educational ladder, the decline in the farm labour force, and the rise in non-farm employment by out-migration (with only one exception that of a storekeeper and moneylender). Out-migration has been to urban areas mainly as teachers, domestic servants, and clerks.

Meanwhile, while the effect of education is not felt in the rural sector, a crude measure of production foregone by the farm family can be ascertained partly in terms of those productive units currently attending an educational institution that are supported out of a part of the net income from farming after deducting payments to labour hired to meet seasonal peaks; and partly in terms of increased output foregone by the diversion of that proportion of consumption expenditures for schooling which could otherwise have been invested in industrial inputs.

It has been conventional among economists to identify scale of production with size of holding, and to proclaim that where land is scarce and holdings small the 'loss' of underemployed family labour constitutes simply the welcome departure of family members who would otherwise only add to leisure but with extra consumption. This, however, is depicting an extreme situation in which the last increments to the labour force have had to depend for subsistence upon the surplus product (that above subsistence needs) of prior increments to the labour force. In the present state of knowledge, and opportunities for applying new inputs which contribute to output increase, scale of production needs redefining. Dalrymple (1971) points out that peculiarly little has been said about 'time' as a possible dimension in evaluating prospects for increasing or improving agricultural output: 'It is possible to make fuller use of time by multiple cropping – the practice of growing more than one crop on the same piece of land in a year.' Intensity of production, as has already been stated, is largely dependent on the availability and efficiency of leading new inputs – those which contribute most to output; and this implies that farmers either have a marketable surplus the proceeds from which they can reinvest, or that they have access to investible funds which they can employ in more labour-intensive productivity raising agricultural practices.

Conversely, in the context of earnings foregone by the student, higher education is many times more costly than elementary education and, as Schultz points out, the rate of return to investment in higher education is grossly over-estimated when earnings foregone are omitted; 'so-called "free" education is far from free to students and their parents, which, in turn, implies that many families with low incomes cannot afford to forego the earnings of their children'.

Schultz (1971) draws attention to the fact that

so-called need is not demand because the concept of demand implies prices and quantities.... The rise in per family income undoubtedly increases the demand for the consumer satisfactions from higher education.... But the demand for the producer component is very hard to determine because it is derived from the production activity of the economy, and because the sources of changes in these derived demands over time are still far from clear.

And, importantly, he adds:

show the highest private rates of return to elementary schooling, and we need to remind ourselves that there are still some children who are not completing the elementary grades. What is more important is the under-investment in the quality of elementary schooling, especially in many rural areas.

Table 11.3 indicates the disproportionately high cost to the farmer in a low-income country compared with the United States of buying

25. Male children in rural Africa walking to the nearest primary school.

26. Elementary school newly opened in Del Monte Resettlement Scheme, Agusan Province, Mindanao.

education for one or more of his children beyond the elementary level. For parents living in rural areas which are remote from large urban centres, there is a considerable element of cost in transport, and in maintenance under urban conditions invariably of inflated prices for home-produced products.

It is clear that the felt want of farmers in the second, third, and fourth 'hand' of farming is primarily for substitutes for family labour; equally, it is clear that the low level of agrochemical inputs, even where irrigation water is available, results in yields which are barely removed from those typical of traditional agriculture practices to meet minimum subsistence requirements.

Here, the problems with which the farmer grapples by reason of his consumption choices, which tend to dictate his production decisions and lead to misallocation of resources, are far more complex than

Hayami and Ruttan (1971) infer in their analysis of resource constraints and technical change. Schultz's 'so-called need' factor among producers as consumers where they are in rural areas isolated by poor communications, partially invalidates the Hayami and Ruttan conclusion that changes in input mixes represent a process of dynamic factor substitution induced primarily by changes in relative factor

27. School leavers in Sarawak on a course at a farmers' training centre.

TABLE 11.3 *Comparative costs of higher education*

Type of education	United States* 1956	Philippines 1970
	Price tags of a year of schooling (Elementary = 1·00)	
Elementary	1·00	1·00
High school	5·07	6·33
College	11·78	40·22†

* Schultz (1971) pp. 126–7: elementary $280, high school $1,420, college $3,300.
† In the capital city of Manila.

28. Mexican farmers meet to receive news of current producer prices offered for their products.

prices. What we are questioning is the presence of such an inducement given poor transport and communications.

As Hayami and Ruttan further point out, the basis for the contrasting patterns of factor price changes is the difference in factor supply conditions; those of the two countries which they examine are that

> in the United States the land supply for agriculture has been more elastic than the labour supply . . . [while] in Japan, the labour supply has been more elastic than the land supply. With the increased demand for farm products in the course of economic development, the price of the less elastic factor tends to rise relative to the prices of the more elastic factors. Given the differences in supply elasticities, agricultural growth in both countries accompanied contrasting changes in land-labor price ratios.

TABLE 11.4   *Land and labour use in a 'dry' farming* (a) *settlement area of Mindanao, Southern Philippines, 1970–71*

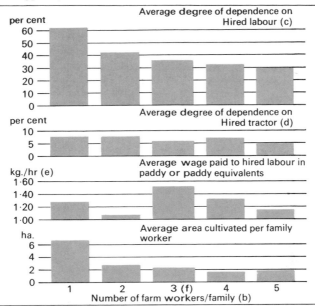

(a) A low labour utilisation economy of extensive agriculture employing draught animals and multiple cropping practices.

(b) The dependancy ratio proportion attributable to family members who have an economic value as farm workers, but who are absent in educational institutions is 0·90 : 1·00; based on the 'statutory' wage rate for farm workers and actual average labour utilisation per adult male of 44·6 per cent, (p.70), production foregone per farm worker at work per annum is estimated at 1·16 metric tons paddy equivalent—representing the cost of hired labour additional to normal practice to replace absent family workers, which must be borne out of gross product.

(c) Transient workers many travelling considerable distances in search of employment.

(d) Owned by private enterprise.

(e) At current market prices the 'statutory' wage rate for farm workers is equivalent to 1·38 kg paddy per hour; the marginal productivity estimate from analysis of human and animal labour used in upland paddy followed by maize is 1·92 kg/hr in paddy equivalents (p.68), and in the particular foodgrain, 0·50 kg paddy/hr, 2·46 kg maize/hr.

(f) The average practice among farm-family households.

In our sample, we have a distorted though not entirely unrelated version of the Hayami and Ruttan thesis; family labour, though family size is large, is affected by the high proportion of absentees in school in the economic age groups, which significantly reduces available work units and, because land substitutes are not fully exploited any more than are labour substitutes to meet a relatively land abundant situation, this also imposes a land constraint.

Table 11.4 illustrates the nature of these constraints, and the degree of substitution for family labour with declining numbers in the work force – which, nevertheless, has not been matched by increased agricultural output such as Hayami and Ruttan associate with the mechanical innovations of a labour-saving type which were induced in the United States, and the biological innovations of a yield-increasing type which were induced in Japan as a result of changes in relative factor prices.

It might be argued that heavier investment in industrial inputs rather than in education for current consumption will not necessarily give rise to increased output from agriculture because of lack of technical knowhow. Yet in all cases among the sample households observed, some damage was recorded from pests and diseases – in many instances causing crop losses of 20 per cent or more – while the higher education which is being purchased at such high cost does not fall into Schultz's third component, namely for skills and knowledge useful in economic endeavour.

TABLE 11.5   *Relative prices in a 'dry' farming area* of Mindanao, Southern Philippines 1970–71*

(Based on paddy = 1·00)

Crop	Diversified holding	Subsistence-type holding
Grains		
Paddy	1·00	1·00
Maize	0·83	0·83
Starchy roots		
Cassava and Sweet Potato	0·48	Not grown
Fruit		
Bananas	0·07	0·07
Citrus	1·52	Not grown
Vegetables		
Egg plant, string beans	0·49	Not grown
Other crops		
Coffee	7·83	Not grown
Coconut	1·22	Not grown

* With the exception of work animals, livestock does not play an important role. Farm family households generally keep a few chicken and pigs, mainly for home consumption and festive occasions.

What perhaps emerges most strongly at this point of discontinuity in agricultural progress is the quite commonly found resistance of small-scale farmers in economically isolated rural areas to any change in technique of production by the application of new input forms apparently because of the risk factor; but this is in large part more because of the consumption oriented structure of their economies.

Table 11.5, which itemises some price relatives, illustrates the gulf between a diversified pattern of production, even in early stages of agricultural development, and the more generally practised low-labour-utilisation subsistence-type production in which farmers cling desperately to the production of staple foodgrains for home consumption; and what we find are built-in virtually self-imposed constraints in the latter sector, which clearly predominate, of which the outward expressions are preoccupation with acquiring aids to lighten physical work and the catastrophic effects of acute sickness among economically active farm family members.

In the ultimate analysis, the real problem with which subsistence-tied producers are faced is that they 'permit' consumption to outstrip production under conditions in which production is starved of investment finance for increased output from agriculture which, even when available, they invariably channel elsewhere.

Part 3
Farming for Profit

CHAPTER 12

Transport and Products

*In practical terms, the community will strive to
market its produce in bulk, at guaranteed prices
agreed upon with the processors. The community
will also strive to acquire its own transport in order
to prevent the middlemen from reaping the benefits
of guaranteed prices by virtue of their monopoly on
transport*
Yitzchak Abt (1971)

'There are two major reasons for emphasising the role of transport in
economic development, more especially in tropical developing
countries. First, transportation is seen as the *sine qua non* of coloniza-
tion, and so, vital in the extension of settlement in a region. . . .
Secondly, and more important, improved and extended transport
facilities are necessary to the widening and fusion of the market in
areas already settled . . .' Is Hodder (1968) implying an employment
generating effect of transport when he states that 'there are great areas
bordering the Amazon Basin now empty of people but which will
prove suitable for settlement when such highways as the Lima–Tonjo
Main Pacific Highway have been constructed'?

It is typical of many countries of the tropics that the construction
of roads have been primarily trunk highways connecting sizeable
towns, and that increased agricultural production from investment in
roads has been largely incidental. The development of internal
transport systems have indeed been notably point-to-point (line haul)
links, and ribbon developments; whereas we may hypothesise that it is
the capillary net with highways radiating from a central city fed by
all-weather feeder roads which offer the greatest scope to the rural
sector for economic development. However, it is no use having a
network of feeder roads without the main roads leading to railways
or markets (or to rivers, for example Irrawaddi). One without the
other gets producers nowhere.

Hardoy (1967) illustrates an aspect of the effects of line haul links
from an examination of the internal structure of Argentine cities,
which have developed spontaneously, with line hauls that are 'totally
inappropriate for achieving a proper interrelation between the

economic locations – industry and commerce, the immediate human habitat – housing and community services, and the basic channels of transportation and communication'.

What Hardoy highlights is that an agrarian and exporting society with a dependent economy requires, and therefore constructs, an urban system different from that of a modern industrial society with a national economy; and he recognises successive stages of urban development moving from the administrative, traditional, and agricultural city, to the modern, industrial and dynamic city.

> The railroads and immigration determined in a few decades the economic orientation of the country and the shape of its urbanisation. . . . The roles which the different urban centres were to play were gradually established within an urban system which defined itself hastily on the basis of the railway lines. . . . In thirty years, forty at most, between 1875 and the first world war, no less than one thousand new localities appeared spontaneously or were founded. In 1914, 332 of these were defined as cities, that is to say that they had more than 2,000 inhabitants. Only three had more than 100,000, only one more than a million. . . . The rural towns at that time were an extension of the open country with which they blended even physically. They were rural groups in almost all their facets. . . . They were little more than intermediate stages in the marketing process between the farm and the dockside silo or cargo ship. In their cultural self-containment and even in their family structure they constituted a requirement of the production and transportation systems in force. The only community service was the school; they lacked other public services such as hospitals. Even the schools reflected through their absentee and dropout ratio the low economic capacity of their rural environment.

The situation which Hardoy describes for the Argentine in earlier decades is typical of much of the tropical world today. By 1920 there were 31,000 km of railway lines in the Argentine; the world of Buenos Aires and the littoral, Hardoy states, has been defined as industrial and modern, the world of the interior as agricultural and traditional. Out of a total population of 7·8 million 25·4 per cent were in Buenos Aires; immigration policies promoted earlier to attract settlers from Northern Europe had failed in the agrarian sector because of the persistence of the *latifundio* (large estates). As Hardoy points out, *latifundio* and large-scale immigration are mutually exclusive. It was inevitable that numerous immigrants would settle in the ports and cities of the coastline where there was employment to be found in building and industrial projects, and opportunities to trade, thus aggravating the geographic isolation of the rural sector.

It has often been said of tropical areas that the intermediary uses the difficulties of both the producer and the retailer, wherever communications in the rural sector are weak, to secure large profits for himself; but may this not rather be a matter of charging the 'right' price for providing intermediary services, where producers have no outlet for marketable surpluses excepting by employing intermediaries' transport to negotiate poorly constructed earth roads which are passable only during the dry season?

The fact that transport investments are typically large hardly needs reiterating; but one of the most neglected factors in the economic development of poor countries is the improvement of earth roads by surfacing with bitumen. 'Engineers consider', states Pedler (1955), 'that the saving of cost in motor transport in West Africa, produced by the improvement of roads, is of the order of 18 per cent when an earth road is given a bitumen surface.' The economic benefits at the producer level are indeed much higher than simply the saving which is reflected in a reduction of the unit cost of motor transport.

The capillary net approach studies the relationship of main and subsidiary roads constructed, as a theoretical goal, within a radius of

29. Vehicle in readiness for government officials leaving the main highway for an earth road feeder link which was impassable by any other means except by a jeep fitted with a winch and wheel chains.

50 km from a sizeable urban consumer centre. However, situations
do occur in which it costs some 30 kg of a staple foodgrain to get one
ton/km of the same product transported; it is clear that to transport
grain to market at this cost over a relatively short distance of 20 km
would be quite out of the question – for the total cost of transport
would have reached 600 kg, or three-fifths of its value.

30. An Iban feast, in an East Malaysian longhouse remote from modern
transport networks.

In practice, where producers have only an earth road, and this
passable for no more than five months of the year in the dry season,
the cost of transporting maize by motor truck (necessarily of limited
capacity because of the state of the roads), has been found by the
writer to reach 42 kg maize equivalent per ton/km of maize transported;
at this unit cost, maize is transported no further than 8 km from the

point of production, by which time expenditure on transport has reached one-third of its value.

Employing data from various sources in Ecuador, Stokes (1968) calculates the effect of upgrading the Santo-Esmeraldas road to a paved all-weather highway to reduce losses of produce through bruising and rotting when transport is interrupted or delayed by bad weather, and production foregone by leaving large quantities of bananas unpicked because of the lack of reliable transportation.

The average daily traffic volume on the unimproved road in 1960 was 200 vehicles. Stokes takes account of 'normal traffic growth' on unimproved highway, 'that which would take place in any case with a road maintained only in its present condition', and assumes an absolute annual increment equal to 5 per cent of 1960 traffic – or ten

31. Wholesaler selling produce bought in the villages off his truck to retailers on reaching the city.

vehicles per day; 'but', he asserts, 'traffic on any improved road will increase annually at a higher rate than normal growth due to the increased development of adjacent land, and output generally, over and above that which would take place normally with the road in its unimproved condition'.

32. Bangkok: river transport bringing produce for sale in the 'Sunday' market.

Stokes made his calculations on the assumption that improvement to the road itself will increase the net output of agriculture from an area extending an average of 2 km on each side traversing fertile agricultural lowlands; and within this zone of influence of 2 km on either side, he estimated that 25 per cent of new land would be brought under cultivation as a direct result of the improved feeder road – equal to a cultivable area of 100 ha per km of road.

Given the improved highway, the producer is still left with the problem of feeding product to the central channel of a highway such as he describes; this is usually by high-cost animal or human transport, or, as has been observed, by 'off the road' vehicles which are expensive. It is this factor which severely limits the zone of influence of a ribbon development.

Furthermore, it is difficult to correlate Stoke's hypothesis with the fact that in many tropical countries there is much uneconomic space, and therefore a need to identify the conditions under which the catalytic effect of transport will pay off, having regard to the alternative demands on scarce resources.

In general, classification systems for roads give no indication of the quality of particular roads, their structure and surfacing, nor the amount of traffic they are carrying; all too frequently they are simply an administrative exercise by persons who almost certainly have never had occasion to travel extensively in the rural sector. Thus a road classified as a main highway may be little more than a 'scraping', and quite incapable of carrying typical unit loads of 10 tons by motor trucks.

Examples of administrative road classifications which provide no indication whatever as to the type of road surface are main, secondary, district, branch, loggers, estate, unclassified; and the disproportionately high cost of 'off-line' transport which keeps small-scale producers virtually subsistence-tied, is totally overlooked by administrators and engineers alike. This leads them to the conclusion that conditions demanding a bituminous surface for feeder roads do not occur.

Surfacing feeder roads with bitumen does, of course, imply a similar, or better, standard in the surfacing of highways, which lends support for the development of capillary net line haul arteries which branch and sub-branch into lesser roads linked by 'ring' roads designed to meet the ideal from the user point of view – that is, that all roads should have a bituminous surfacing.

It has been said in the United States that any concentration of population of less than 2,500 is uneconomic for adequate servicing, and that this figure should therefore be regarded as the lowest common denominator. The capillary net approach to infrastructural development to the standard which we are discussing is inevitably heavily dependent on topography and terrain, the value of output from land, 'exportable surpluses', and a twoway traffic of people and products from a central town or city. An important consideration is backload from urban to rural areas of consumer goods, but with poor farmers to buy, this may be below capacity so that lorries run half empty on one journey adding to costs to the farmer, unless the value/weight of the backload is much higher than that of the farm produce transported.

For infrastructural development, locating these centres of potential growth implies acceptance of the principle that concentration is the starting point for the policy of establishing social and economic services in rural areas.

In the Mexican *Mesa Central*, however, it would appear that ribbon development of a super-highway has in fact acted as a catalyst for a group of farmers in the small town of San Lucas el Grande, who are selling fresh vegetables daily in Mexico City – a distance of 85 km. This community has established a reputation for supplying a large quantity of the City's vegetables: 80 tons per day of onions, tomatoes, lettuce, carrots, chillies, and quash (pumpkin). A few of the more enterprising of the local people own ten-ton capacity trucks; they load up each afternoon and leave at night for Mexico City. By pooling their produce and organising their own transport, taking advantage of the exceptionally good road conditions, they are able to keep transport costs low – in terms of the local price of maize at the time of the writer's observations (July 1971) 0·68 kg maize equivalent per ton/km, or a total cost of 58 kg (5·8 per cent).

If transport costs had been higher, the trucking of vegetables might have been prohibitive, since they are a high-cost product in labour and

33. Mexican farmer earthing up his maize crop using a horse-drawn implement.

industrial inputs, and perishability and handling losses make vegetables a high-risk product. Even at this low transport cost, however,
there is considerable argument over prices.

Projected sufficiency levels for vegetables fall far short of requirements in virtually all densely urbanised areas of the tropics. Yet the
producer often leaves his product to rot 'because prices are too low';
'last week's quash prices were too low', they said in San Lucas el

34. Small-scale irrigation works employing self-help methods transforms a
Mindanao settlement into a high farming area.

Grande – only 13·8 per cent of the value of a similar weight of
maize – so they 'did not sell and this is wastage'. The cost of transporting quash to Mexico City at the price offered would have meant a
sevenfold increase in terms of maize equivalent, totalling 406 kg – over
40 per cent taken up in transport, and all the evidence points to the

fact that whenever transport costs exceed one-third of the gross value of the product farmers do not sell.

It is therefore unrealistic to pay much attention to the low transport costs over this stretch, which consists almost entirely of super-highway, in terms of maize unless the vegetables offered for sale have a price relative at least equal to that of maize or higher.

35. The Royal Thai Government establishes vegetable growers with good access to water, all-weather roads and markets: first produced Haswell (1972).

Most of the farmers of San Lucas el Grande come within the fold of Mexico's Land Reform measures, and are *ejidos* enjoying *de facto* tenure of approximately 2·5 ha per family. It is a 'dry' area, however, entirely planted to maize, and a one-crop season lasting for 270 days from planting to harvesting; yields are generally poor, attributed mainly to deficient rainfall during the growing season; scarcities

36. The author (behind) and her helpers on a data collecting exercise in Mindanao.

result which cause the price to rise sharply in off-season periods, and producers suffer hardship when they are faced with buying maize for home consumption to meet a 'hungry season' gap.

Nevertheless, this community has brought a proportion of the land under irrigation, employing self-help methods in the construction of a small dam and five wells, and so they are able to cultivate vegetables as a subsidiary crop; but their plea is for massive irrigation works capable of converting their one-season corn land to a multiple-cropping system. There is much discussion; they are astute and alert; they seek a progressive agriculture which will enable them to develop within their own environs with less dependence on a remote capital city for their cash sales, which leaves them little better off than the minimum for subsistence. However, as Folke Dovring (1969) points out:

> private farms in Mexico are still the dominant part of the country's agriculture. . . . *Ejidos* were created mainly where population was dense. Private farmers therefore retained most of the land in the most sparsely settled areas of the country. This arrangement left them with the lion's share not only of the nation's pastures and wastes but also of its virgin land resources. The larger share in virgin land also explains why private farmers now have a larger share in the irrigated land in the country.

The availability of fertile irrigated land north of Mexico City has attracted private investment in agro-industries – particularly private foreign investment in the canning industry – both for export and supplying a far from saturated demand for fruit and vegetables in Mexico's urban sector; this has encouraged intensification of farming under the new irrigation systems which have followed programmes of land clearance.

Private foreign investment in particular to secure a favourable export market has depended on the management's ability to provide supporting services wherever the rural community is too small, or too disorganised, to serve as an economic unit. For processing plants can centralise; they are set within the framework of a sophisticated industrial technology operating with highly skilled manpower; and they have the economic strength to exert some pressure for improvement in infrastructural development.

But transport costs are at least eight times greater than rates paid by San Lucas el Grande's self-appointed group of producers supplying fresh vegetables daily to Mexico City 85 km from the producing area. The maximum economic radius of operation from the processing plant, privately communicated to the writer by one such industry, is 100 km whatever the class of road. Unless producer prices are high relative to maize, at this transport cost such a radius of operation would be quite untenable if the producer were to bear the total cost of transport.

Dealing entirely in fruit and vegetables – peas, string beans, tomatoes, garlic, onions, beans, and peaches – the processor contracts with growers, and for the 'right product' pays a high price, but penalises the grower heavily for 'off-grade' produce; for example, when contracting for tender peas, producer prices are substantially reduced if peas are too tender or too hard.

Some share of the cost of transport will inevitably be borne by the industry, and passed on to the consumer. These user's costs include taxation, and operating costs – fuel consumption, repairs and maintenance, labour and parts. User's cost will fall with any improvement to a road, because of lower fuel consumption and costs of repairs and maintenance, particularly tyre wear; user's cost should also fall with improvement to a road because it will have the effect of generating traffic each unit of which should receive in benefit more than it costs. Assuming that a tax is imposed, the net gain to a country from generated traffic may also be expected to be reflected in a reduction of the tax element of user's costs, although there should be an overall gain in public sector revenue from generated traffic; and because of time savings, and reduction in the proportion of fatal and serious accidents which are commonly associated with gravel and earth roads despite lower traffic flows.

C. A. Jackson (1971), presenting a paper on the Tomato Canning

Industry in Nigeria, drew attention to the host of practical problems with which an 'infant' agro-industry is faced in tropical countries, 'not least of which is the problem of transporting tomatoes over tracks one would not normally consider suitable for a tank'; should we expect producers to adopt improved techniques of production and be willing to outlay quite substantial amounts of capital, or raise credit, for industrial inputs, when infra-structure is so weak and the marketing system inadequate?

This 3,000 ton capacity processing plant has been established in Zaria in North Central State for local puree production, which, on present (1971) yields (12·3 tons average/tomatoes/hectare), represents 244 ha (three times the present area under tomatoes).

> It is doubtful that we can attain this acreage (hectarage) under the present conditions where we rely on small areas from 2–25 acres (0·8–10 hectares) spread over a forty-mile (64 km) radius. We are told that within the next two years the Government will complete several large irrigation schemes within a reasonable distance of our factory, and if this in fact happens, then we should be able to obtain all the tomatoes we need. . . . Water at the recommended interval would double yields (Jackson, 1971).

Where no local abbatoire and cold storage facility exists, the cost of transporting cattle in response to a demand for meat in urban areas virtually prices this product out of the market. Areas suitable for grazing ranch cattle are found in Mindanao, southern Philippines, where population densities are low.

The transportation costs for one such ranch are shown in Table 12.1, and clearly indicate the magnitude of this problem. Patently this cost is too great for the average small-scale producer to bear. They represent costs incurred by a ranch of many thousand hectares, with a stocking capacity of one head of cattle per hectare; cattle graze for fifteen days grasses which then take thirty days to recover. No other feed is given, but the cattle are provided with iodine and salt licks, and have access to 'plenty of nice creeks'.

This ranch is rented jointly by a number of industrial corporations, and is in the charge of a resident manager. The extremely low rental paid suggests that there is no alternative use for the land – that is to say, that the opportunity cost is zero. But local 'political' disturbances do arise from time to time with their concomitant problems of security of tenure in the region generally; and there has been extensive 'rustling' of animals by indigenous 'slash-and-burn' cultivators in this sparsely populated area.

Rufener (1971) tells an anecdote on the fate of stolen animals:

> Robert Gurevich, a doctoral candidate from the University of Pittsburgh, studied during 1970 the various roles played by school teachers in Thai

village life. Among his acquaintances were several teachers from a village renowned for its lawlessness. According to the teachers, meat consumption in that particular village was considerably higher than in more ordinary places. The teachers explained that people in their village were frequently awakened late at night by men carrying freshly killed beef. Villagers were told that they would buy a certain portion at a fixed price. Duress was implicit, as was the assumption that the meat was contraband from stolen animals.

We may, however, hypothesise that a main reason for there being no alternative use for the land in the Northern Cotabato region other than extensive grazing of beef cattle is the deplorable state of the roads. The transportation of agricultural products over some 250 km of rough roads northwards before an outlet for marketable surpluses

TABLE 12.1   *The cost of transporting beef cattle from Northern Cotabato, Mindanao, to Manila meat market*

	Per cent of Producer price (*April, 1970*) ex-ranch
OVERLAND TRANSPORT	
Commercial motor truck in Mindanao	3·3
(maximum capacity: 12 head of cattle)	
188 km over unsurfaced road to depository, where fed for two weeks on commercial grasses to recover loss in weight.	
68 km over unsurfaced road to port of exit	
WATERBORNE TRANSPORT	
Commercial ship from Mindanao Island to Manila in Central Luzon	8·0
	——
	11·3
Three days' journey to Manila depository, where held for one week for fattening (but only recover about one-quarter of weight loss)	
MAINTENANCE COSTS IN MINDANAO AND MANILA DEPOSITORIES	15·2
	——
	26·5
NET WEIGHT LOSS IN VALUE TERMS	15·0
	——
	41·5
	==
Average liveweight at time of sale in Manila	255kg
Price relatives (maize in Mindanao = 1·00)	
Local sales of cattle ex-ranch (liveweight)	2·02
Manila price for cattle transported (liveweight)	4·39
Manila price, less cost of transportation (including weight loss)	2·08
Profit margin over local sales ex-ranch	3·0%

can be found, is not conducive to the creation of a diversified agriculture and market-oriented farmers; such conditions are a positive
disincentive to immigration on any large scale, which would otherwise
occur spontaneously to meet the economic challenge of the availability of fertile lands with high development potential.

In fact, in this region an obvious outlet is westward to Cotabato
city – a distance of 80 km; but the first 25 km of road is impassable
by commercial vehicles, which not only acts as an effective barrier
to economic development, but in addition so isolates producers that
they fall easy prey to lawlessness, and the 'profiteering' of local
storekeepers and millowners. These are usually one and the same person
who 'buys paddy after harvest from the producers and sells back to
them later milled rice from which he secures a profit margin of at
least 65 per cent; simultaneously, the producers obtain from his store
such items as Liberty tinned milk to which he adds a minimum of
10 per cent to the retail price'.

What is the evidence from surveys of felt wants at producer level?
Priorities voiced by communities wherever subsistence-tied farmers
form the majority of the populace are nowhere very different.
Highest is generally for roads, even in relatively densely populated
areas where feeder links are weak or non-existent, with consequent
deleterious effects on producer prices. Second is invariably for land
surveys:

> within the fragmented and scattered structure of their holdings, peasant
> producers spread the risks of crop failure. If one plot receives too much
> water and the crop is damaged or destroyed, another will have sufficient,
> in any one season. Their strong resistance to attempts to consolidate
> holdings may be partly explained by this deeply entrenched mini-altitude
> pattern of behaviour in their planning decisions.

Levelling is a task beyond the scope of the small-scale producer,
without which irrigation facilities, even if they exist, will not be fully
exploited for higher income levels from increased productivity of
labour and of land.

Thirdly, the felt want is mainly for better health: access to modern
medicines and treatment, and safe drinking water. Almost all other
felt wants are subject to these three primary constraints.

The adverse effects on living standards are not only that they
impose severe checks on the *means* of production; but also on its
most important component: the *motive* for production.

CHAPTER 13

Employment and Trade

Even though you have 10,000 fields, you can only
eat one measure of rice a day. . . .' Chinese Wisdom

What is the evidence that improvement in agricultural techniques, of which irrigation is the most powerful, will exert a strong upward pull on the demand for agricultural labour?

In 1916, Slater (1918) found in Eruvellipet, a South Arcot District village in South India, that payment to *padials*, or serfs, was 412 kg paddy per year – 1·13 kg paddy per day, or 'one measure of rice a day', whether or not work was available. In 1961 payment to landless agricultural labourers was 440 kg per year for an average of 131 days on which work was available; at this period, many landholders were applying fertilisers and irrigation water, and were able to produce 440 kg on an area as small as 0·126 hectares.

In Dusi, a North Arcot District village, the average wage paid to agricultural hired labour in 1961 for a day's work was 3·34 kg paddy; here there was greater diversification of crop production, and this resulted in an average of 180 days on which work was available, or a total wage of 600 kg paddy per agricultural worker per year. Fifty years earlier, however, Slater had observed that price exerted a significant influence in this village because of its accessibility to a large urban and commercial centre (Haswell, 1967).

Prafulla Sanghvi (1969) states the case for population pressure on land 'reducing the areas of an increasing number of holders to such an extent that they are compelled to depend on wage-labour in agriculture as their main source of livelihood. . . . In Bengal, the real wage-rate in terms of rice fell from 2·783 seers (2·60 kg) in 1852 to between 1·250 (1·16 kg) and 1·875 seers (1·75 kg) in 1922'. Assuming a 35 per cent milling loss, these real wage rates are equivalent to 4·00 kg, 1·80 kg, and 2·70 kg paddy respectively. Sanghvi further observes that

in the past, the system of mutual exchange of labour played an important role in meeting labour requirement during the harvesting period. The difference in times of sowing and in the crop-pattern of the individual cultivators enabled them to help each other during the harvesting period. A fairly equitable distribution of land among all persons dependent on agriculture is an essential pre-condition for the proper functioning of this system. This pre-condition disappeared on account of the emergence and growth of landless agricultural workers and inequality in distribution of land among owner and tenant cultivators. The disappearance of the pre-condition and growth of a money economy led to the gradual disintegration of the system of mutual exchange of labour, although its survivals are found in some villages to this day.

For tropical regions in general, Sanghvi's observation that there has been a disappearance of mutual exchange of labour cannot be substantially supported; but he is referring to Bengal, a notorious example of extreme population pressure leading to excessive fragmentation of holdings, particularly where all the sons of large families remain at home to swell the ranks of the underemployed. Nevertheless, in a low-income economy in which the majority of workers are in agriculture, and there is a surplus of urban as well as rural labour, growth rates cannot be accelerated simply by transferring labour from agriculture to industry and manufacture. Unless the productivity of the agricultural sector is raised at the same time so that a larger number of non-agricultural workers can be fed, their transfer will not be possible.

Raanan Weitz (1971) reinforces this argument with a comparison of output between the farmer and the industrial worker which, in certain countries, is 'on a scale of 2 to 1, or even 3 to 1. . . . Only when the farm family produces far more than it consumes is the surplus converted into purchasing power for non-agricultural commodities. . . . A further result of the lag in agricultural productivity is the inability of agriculture to meet the growing demand for food of an increasing non-agricultural population'; and, in consequence, the large share of limited resources which has to be set aside for imports of food.

Of particular importance is the attention given by Weitz to those countries where there is no surplus manpower in rural areas – a factor which is frequently lost sight of because of the overwhelming problems of rural areas which have high rates of under and unemployed persons.

In those countries where there is no surplus manpower in rural areas, especially in Africa, there is the further problem of the shift of workers from agriculture to other sectors. Any such transfer of labor that is not accompanied by increased efficiency of agricultural production impairs the productive capacity of the agricultural sector and reduces still further its ability to meet the demands made upon it.

Table 13.1 illustrates the magnitude of this problem when a government wishes to exploit underutilised resources in a labour scarce, land abundant, situation. If rates of wages paid in each category of non-agricultural employment can be equated with the marginal value productivity of that enterprise, then Weitz's reference to the difference in output between the farmer and the industrial worker is substantially true also of the State of Sarawak. But to what extent can it be said of Sarawak, as Weitz has stated as a general principle, that 'while extraordinary investment is continuously being made in technological improvements in industry, the agricultural worker is left to carry on with out-moded methods of production'?

Figures contained in Tables 13.1 and 13.2 are an indication of the supply price of labour of which the supply price of labour for logging and its associated manufacturing sector is of particular importance. Theoretically, the supply price of labour indicates its highest contribution to output, which in turn reflects its economic scarcity.

Past experience in Africa has been that where there is relative isolation caused by low population densities farmers have tended to practise extensive rather than intensive methods of cultivation to meet home consumption needs, with little or no increase in yield per unit of area. Labour peaks occur, however, in subsistence production; and these immobilise labour in terms of sheer numbers of workers in so far as there can be no reduction in the labour force in agriculture

TABLE 13.1 *Non-agricultural sector wages relative to agricultural wages: State of Sarawak, East Malaysia, 1968*

Employment	Non-agricultural wage relative to agricultural wage	No. of employees as per cent of total employed
AGRICULTURAL WAGE WORKERS	1·00	2·1
Other primary industries	2·35	10·5
Manufacturing	1·97	40·2
Construction	1·70	6·4
Electricity, gas, water	2·90	2·3
Banks and finance	3·55	0·8
Transport and communication	2·37	4·7
Services	1·95	33·0
All industries	2·02	100·0
Total population		950,000
Urban population, per cent		21
Rural population, per cent		79
Per cent of total population in wage employment		4·1

TABLE 13.2 *Main sectors of wage employment in primary and manufacturing industries, 1968*

Industry	Wage relative to agriculture	No. of employees as per cent of total employed
Primary industries (excluding agriculture)		
Logging	2·26	69·4
Crude petroleum, natural gas	3·96	12·1
Quarrying	1·97	11·7
Manufacturing		
Foodstuffs	1·16	4·4
Textiles	0·84	1·3
Sawmills, planing mills, etc.	2·17	68·3
Rubber products	1·18	1·5
Metal products	1·53	1·6

SOURCE: Data abstracted from the *Annual Bulletin of Statistics: State of Sarawak*, Sarawak, East Malaysia, 1967–68.

unless there is a fundamental change in cultural practice, or alternatively food import. It is the quality of this labour force that should further engage our attention for it is frequently heavily weighted with women, older men, and children; younger men who have remained in the village are usually only part-time farmers.

We may recall Norman's (1970) study which shows a significant increase in the weighted average in one village of days worked by adult males from 140 on the farm to 263 in total per year when he takes account of other occupations whether they be 'jobs that have been carried out for many generations', or those that have arisen 'directly or indirectly as a result of improved communications and the development of large cities, commercial firms, and governmental bodies'. This dichotomy has to be recognised; while economists plan for the most profitable combination of enterprises and optimal patterns of resource use, the development potential of agriculture is dependent on the investment decisions of farmers and their response to economic incentives, which in turn are subject to a multitude of other factors within the farm-family structure; these do not necessarily have a direct bearing on agricultural production, but rather make conflicting demands upon the time and energies of farm-family households.

A fundamental change in cultural practice implies the transfer of labour out of subsistence production, and the application of hired labour to cash crops, including food crops on which it should also be profitable to use that labour.

Clayton (1963) refers to the condition on family farms in Nyeri District in Kenya which employ no labour in a situation in which 'in general, it is labour not land which limits increased production'. What is invariably overlooked in the conversion to cash crop production is, however, aptly expressed by Clayton:

> A constricting consequence of family labour arises because farming systems in Kenya include high-value cash crops such as coffee, tea and pyrethrum. These crops are very labour-demanding; for example, coffee requires about four times as much labour as maize. One of the effects of this is that farm families can achieve maximum annual profits only when some of their land is left uncropped.

For the group of holdings in his study, Clayton states that 'the use of hired labour substantially increases farm incomes'. But in any area which is relatively isolated from the market economy in which family members are engaged primarily in subsistence production, the opportunity cost of off-season labour is low. Platt (1946) found this to be 0·35 kg maize equivalent per man hour for cotton in the northern and central regions of Malawi in 1939, and later findings by the writer confirmed this general figure for subsistence production.

In 1968, however, relatively large-scale cotton producers in the southern region of Malawi were found to be applying hired labour on a regular basis at a wage of 2·15 kg maize equivalent per man hour, because 'cotton pays and it is better to stay here than go to Rhodesia'. This is consistent with the long-run opportunity cost quoted by other workers for East Africa, which range between 2·00 and 2·7 kg maize equivalent per man hour. In other words, 2·15 kg maize equivalent per man hour was the most that Malawian labour was able to command when working for local farmers, which therefore tended to be the minimum cost at which this factor of production could be obtained by cotton producers. If the farmer could not pay that wage in the long run, he would not get labour.

Similarly, in Sarawak's land abundant labour scarce Fourth Division, the most favourable price labour can command is when working for logging companies, which therefore tends to be the minimum cost at which this factor of production can be obtained; and in any programme of agricultural development which the state or other body may wish to launch to bring unutilised resources into production, unless they as employers of labour are prepared to pay this wage they will not get labour.

Sarawak still has huge untapped resources in timber and it may be questioned whether investments which are applied to an agriculture dependent on an abundant supply of labour may not be wasted when the going wage between the agricultural worker and other primary industry workers is on a scale of more than 2 to 1. In these circumstances it would be totally unrealistic to operate as if the opportunity cost of labour is zero, which is not the case. It is not the gap between the wages and the short-run productivity of the raw labour that is paramount, but the attraction of labour into the agricultural industry by raising wages while simultaneously promoting means of economising labour and raising its productivity.

Both cash crops – rubber, pepper, and coconuts – and the staple foodgrain paddy, are heavily subsidised by the state government of Sarawak; yet the level of inputs, other than land and labour which are traditional, remains low. As we should expect in these circumstances, the level of output of paddy is also low, being consistent with that generally found among peasant producers cultivating by traditional methods under natural conditions of soil and water; and there is food import. For example, weeding and harvesting have to be completed within a quite limited period if yields are not to suffer. They are also highly labour-intensive operations, and frequently the family does not have sufficient labour available to complete them within the optimal period.

It is not only paddy which is labour demanding, but also rubber and pepper, all of which impose a labour constraint, and only those with large families or who are able to hire labour can cultivate more than one of these crops. Even with the inclusion of cash crops, however, the evidence points to a return to family labour comparable only with that of an unskilled labourer's wage, which offers no incentive for entrepreneurial activity; and the innovatory age group among the economically active members of the population are attracted into other primary industries and manufacturing, or they migrate to take up wage employment elsewhere, notably in Brunei.

Equally, in countries with densely populated rural areas wherever farm families are living near the minimum for subsistence, wages have to be relatively high to attract labour into the wage economy. Some of the underlying factors here which render labour supply inelastic at the subsistence wage are lack of basic physical stamina caused by malnutrition and disease which induces apathy, and adjustment to the industrial discipline of having to work regularly and continuously.

The phenomenon of open seasonal unemployment in low-income rural areas, particularly where they are dominated by a monocropping system with its peaks and troughs of labour demand, is well known; but Fuchs and Vingerhoets (1971) point to the obvious fact that 'in traditional agriculture always *some* work can be done'. In the context of the imbalance between the share of the agricultural and non-agricultural employment sectors, however (78·3 and 21·7 per cent respectively in Thailand in 1969), it is the relation between the increase in production of the non-agricultural sector and the increase in the number of persons which it employs which is of particular importance. Fuchs and Vingerhoets state this for Thailand:

> The output (value added) of the non-agricultural sectors increased on average by almost 9·5 per cent per annum between 1960 and 1969. Employment generated by these sectors during the same period amounts to an increase of between 4·6 and 4·7 per cent per annum. These figures imply that an increase in output of the non-agricultural sectors of 1 per cent was accompanied by an increase of employment in these sectors of about 0·5 per cent.

We are further reminded by them of the well-known fact that farmers in Thailand, as has been observed in many other countries which have large proportions of their populations in the rural sector, 'succeed in topping their income from the farm by activities outside farming'. Based on data drawn from the National Statistical Office survey on income and expenditure of farmers (1963), Fuchs and Vingerhoets estimate that Thai farmers succeed in finding off-farm employment which adds about 15 per cent to their agricultural income. In essence, however, the agricultural sector has remained largely traditional.

The very nature of the problem of low productivity agricultures and the concomitant evils of the rural poor whose numbers relentlessly press in upon already overcrowded underserviced cities, surely lies in the inability of governments and their peoples to escape from that point of discontinuity which occurs at the 'fourth hand of farming' – the point at which some use is made of water resources but cultivation remains largely either by hand hoe or assisted by draft animals without the aid of industrial inputs.

That this point of discontinuity has been reached by almost all low-income rural sectors of Third World countries is an undeniable fact. To raise the level of agricultural productivity to that enjoyed in the 'fifth and sixth hand' of farming requires that there shall be a decisive *pull* towards the agricultural industry; but in practice, when all the emphasis should be on entry into the wider economy which a modernised agricultural industry demands, the pull is sociologically and psychologically everywhere away from agriculture which continues to be identified with subsistence-tied production.

The length and severity of the period between the third and fourth 'hand' has become the most acute, and the underlying causes are basically the non-alignment of institutional structures, and the transport and communications gap.

The 'fifth hand of farming' adds the use of fertilizer and insecticides.

Scoville, in an unpublished paper on farm and agribusiness relationships in economic development, calls attention to an attempt to
project manpower needs in terms of specific activities, and remarks
that 'for each of several important farm inputs the numbers of
skilled and unskilled workers is estimated for each phase of production or distribution of a given level of output'; but these are somewhat
unrealistic in the sense that the theorists persist in oversimplifying and
understating the potential share of agribusiness in national income
and employment; the inclusion of manpower estimates for farm
product processing and distribution activities to give total manpower
estimates for the agribusiness sector is needed for a more refined
knowledge of the contribution of farm modernisation to expansion of
this sector.

A proposal for the establishment of a combined producer-transit-
wholesaler market complex serving terminal food markets in strategic
population centres in the Philippines offers a useful illustration of the
importance of vegetables in relation to total food supply and imbalances between supply and demand.

Since most vegetable growers are engaged in small-scale production,
most pre-sale practices are primitive; the main constraint is shortage
of capital which prevents farmers from undertaking the additional
cost of labour and equipment needed for more sophisticated pre-
marketing preparation of produce. In general, no grading or sizing is
done; tomatoes, for example, are simply classified as ripe or unripe.
Packing is done manually, leafy vegetables being packed in bamboo
baskets.

The farmer sells his vegetables to a local (first) buyer who usually main-
tains contact with several farmers in the area. The produce is passed on
to a buyer (trucker merchant), who in turn transports the harvest to a
market center like Manila where he sells to wholesalers. The Manila
wholesalers dispose of their supply to so-called jobbers (secondary
wholesalers) or to retailers. The jobbers in turn sell to retailers usually
composed of market vendors. These retailers may deliver to other
retailers who handle the final link in the distribution chain.

The Greater Manila Food Market report states that some light was
shed following a survey in 1968 on the extent and source of capital
involved in the production of vegetables in Mountain Province;
'non-bank lenders supplied 60 per cent of farmers' capital investments
while the farmers themselves put up only 31 per cent. The contribution of banks amounted to only 9 per cent of the total.'

Apart from suitability of soils and climatic considerations, degree
of perishability dictates supply where vegetables originate in areas at
some distance from the market. In the Manila market, cabbage is the
only item that accounts for a significant proportion (17 per cent) of

TABLE 13.3   *Trained manpower requirements for industrial inputs*

Kind of Input	Unit of input	Activity	Workers required per unit No. skilled	No. unskilled
Fertiliser	1,000 m. tons of nutrients produced and distributed	production wholesale retail total	1 1 1 3	1 1 3 5
Seed processing	3,000 m. tons capacity	production and warehousing marketing and distribution administrative research and development total	2 5 2 1 10	5 3 2 1 11
Pesticides	1,000 m. tons, technical grade, production	manufacturing formulation research education regulation total	3 1 13 9 6 32	n.a.
Tractor mechanisation	12,000 tractors with related equipment produced per year	manufacture	450	700
Power tillers	10,000 units produced per year	manufacture	500	720
Animal-drawn equipment	100,000 moldboard plows and other equipment produced per year	manufacture	250	500
Power dusters and sprayers	30,000 knapsack and 4,000 tractor sprayers per year	manufacture	70	150

SOURCE: President's Science Advisory Committee, *The World Food Problem*, Washington, 1967, iii, 114–207; quoted by Scoville, p. 15.

TABLE 13.4 *Marketing projections: Greater Manila and surrounding areas*

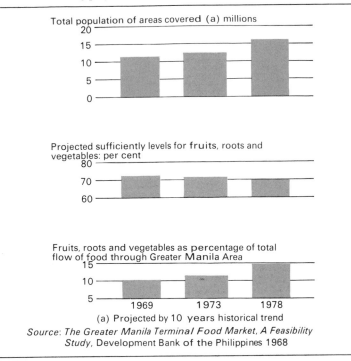

Total population of areas covered (a) millions

Projected sufficiently levels for fruits, roots and vegetables: per cent

Fruits, roots and vegetables as percentage of total flow of food through Greater Manila Area

(a) Projected by 10 years historical trend

Source: *The Greater Manila Terminal Food Market, A Feasibility Study*, Development Bank of the Philippines 1968

total supply, although green corn and egg plant, in addition to cabbage, rank high in availability.

Cernohous (1966) has observed that while a price decline tends to be reflected at the lower stages of the marketing channel very rapidly, price increases usually seep down gradually and tend to be retained within the channel so that the farmer benefits not only last but least. 'These conditions apparently tend to peg the average prices paid to producers considerably below their "competitive" level, discouraging an efficient resource allocation, and depressing producers' incomes below what they might be under a more efficient marketing system.' Most marked price disturbances generally occur in the market of vegetables, which are nevertheless not brought about solely by an inefficient distribution system, but also by seasonal and climatic factors.

This tale of the influence in the market of a large unsatisfied demand being reduced by lack of storage and freezing facilities to offset seasonality factors, a poor distribution system, costly interruptions in transport, and climatic hazards, is epitomised by Ranaan Weitz (1971):

> Travelling in southern Turkey several years ago, I found that the prices of vegetables and fruit rose continuously as I proceeded from the farm to the stall in the village, to the market in the nearby town, to the wholesale market in the capital, and to the greengrocer's store in a residential suburb, where the prices were 200 to 250 per cent higher than at the farm gate.

Rhind caps Weitz's observation with another of his own: 'The price differential between producer and retailer is just as marked in Europe as in Asia. In Italy in 1971 our apples were 50 lira at the gate at harvest and 180 lira in the village shop half a kilometre away.'

This begs the question as to what economic incentives small-scale producers really have to purchase industrial inputs, and apply large additions of labour to that traditionally used on subsistence crops? Can they be expected to engage in the intensive cultivation of vegetables on a commercial basis when infrastructure is so weak and the market system inadequate?

Table 13.5 clearly indicates the labour intensive characteristic of the vegetable industry. 'The contribution to farm efficiency of scale economies compared to personal attention varies among different crops and livestock branches and in different stages of development', Weitz states, and 'generally speaking, the more individual attention a branch of farming needs, the more suitable it will be for a family farm'. In this category he places dairy and vegetable farming. When however there exists a fast and efficient road network, as for example in the Central Plain of Thailand where there is heavy concentration on fruit and vegetable truck farming to supply the Bangkok market, the vegetable industry can no longer be regarded as a family farm business in the strict sense of an earlier stage of development in which capital is scarce and labour abundant. Intensity of labour requirements is shown to be three to four times those of the traditional family farm – beyond the scope of the family farm without some hiring of labour especially for land preparation, labour in planting, maintenance, and harvesting.

The commercial production of vegetables to high standards of quality and packing also requires substantial outlays of capital, or the availability of credit for industrial inputs. Legumes are particularly important in the diet of rice-eating peoples; but although the price relative shown in Table 13.5 for string beans is comparatively high, so also is the level of input of fertilisers, insecticides, and fungicides high, and the additional cost of labour and materials required for erecting trellises, sorting and grading at harvest, and packing.

TABLE 13.5 *Employment-generating effect of the production* of vegetables for commercial sale in terminal food markets to high standards of quality, grading, and packaging*

	Gross product per man hour (revised estimates)	Proportion of gross value of product expended on fertilisers, insecticides, and fungicides	Intensity of labour requirement (Traditional practice = 1·0)	Price relative to paddy = 1·00
	kg paddy equivalent	%		
Leafy vegetables				
Chinese cabbage	3·83	28·9	3·7	0·88
Pechay†	8·92	19·8	3·0	0·66
Fruit vegetables				
Egg plant‡	10·59	7·7	3·1	0·33
Tomatoes	8·09	11·7	2·9	0·88
Pepper§ (sweet)	6·09	14·4	3·3	0·66
Legumes				
String beans	2·35	42·5	3·2	1·55
		Traditional practice‖		
All locally grown vegetables (including egg plant and string beans)	4·73	—	1·0	0·33

* Calculated from revised estimates of the cost of production of specific products contained in *Vegetable Financing Program*, Development Bank of the Philippines, February 1968.
† *Brassica pekinensis* Linn.
‡ *Solanum melongena* Linn.
§ *Capsicum annum. var. grossum* (Linn.) Sandt.
‖ Calculated from 1970 measurements of labour input and product output from garden plots in an area of Mindanao where vegetables can be grown on a year-round basis.

Furthermore, for successful production of vegetables an assured water supply is basic; but, as Duckham and Masefield (1970) point out,

> the intensity of farming systems in the tropics is often determined not by the natural environment but by the density of the human population. In a subsistence economy, denser human populations must tend to produce smaller individual farms and at the same time a greater abundance of farm labour, thus inducing more intensive production from the land whether or not it is best suited for such use. The extreme case is a Chinese

farmer with less than an acre of land, whose farming becomes indistinguishable from horticulture and who may take five or six crops of vegetables a year, fertilising them largely with human excreta and watering them manually, irrespective of the soil type or rainfall.

Fertiliser consumption which has transformed Japanese smallholdings into viable units in which, though income expenses necessary for earning gross income are large net incomes are high, has not been generally repeated in tropical regions of the world. Heseltine (1965) recorded in 1958 that Japan showed the highest world consumption of fertilising elements $(N + P_2O_5 + K_2O)$ per hectare of arable land, averaging 246 kg, compared with 204 kg in the Netherlands, 149 kg in West Germany, 53 kg in the United Kingdom, 13 kg in the United States of America, and 1·5 kg in India. Japan pioneered the use of fertilisers on irrigated paddy fields; by 1940 fertiliser consumption was 9·3 times that of 1903.

TABLE 13.6   *Rates of fertiliser consumption by world regions 1969/70*

Region	All fertiliser nutrients* per hectare of arable land and land under permanent crops (kg)
Europe	158
North and Central America	66
U.S.S.R.	35
Oceania	33
Mainland China	30
Asia	22
South America	14
Africa	7

SOURCE: *Monthly Bulletin of Agricultural Economics and Statistics*, FAO, vol 20, February 1971.
* Arable land and land under permanent crops include land under temporary crops (double-cropped areas are counted only once), land temporarily fallow, temporary meadows, land under market and kitchen gardens, land under fruit trees, nut trees, vines, rubber, coffee, etc.

In Thailand, for example, the lag in yield increases has been associated with the slow progress in adoption of fertiliser (4·9 kg of fertilising elements $N + P_2O_5 + K_2O$ per ha in 1966–67). Fertilisers are much more expensive in the tropics than in the West. Also it is not known how best to use them.

Kolshus (1972) found under modernisation of paddy farming in Northeast Thailand that on the average 1 kg of fertiliser adds about 5 kg of rice to the yield under farm conditions. His general hypothesis is that profitability does affect the rate at which farmers learn about new technology and influences their decision to adopt or reject the innovation; but that other factors also play a role in determining how rapidly and to what degree farmers respond to a given economic opportunity. At the rice and fertiliser prices prevailing at the time of the study,

> the ratio of the marginal value product of fertilizer to the cash price of fertilizer was calculated to be about 2·5, an objective indicator that fertiliser is profitable under existing field conditions. The ratio is, however, very sensitive to changes in input and output prices, as well as the terms of credit the farmers can obtain if fertiliser is not paid for in cash. This was especially the case among farmers who exhibited behaviour consonant with a production goal of consumption sufficiency. Farmers who marketed a substantial amount of their production were found to use significantly more fertilizer than other farmers.

The added yield due to fertiliser use was found to be 'less than dramatic in terms of percentage increase. The average amount of fertiliser used was found to add about 12 per cent to the yield.' This was apparently not enough to convince the farmer of its profitability. Importantly, Kolshus found indication of 'risk sensitivity': 'farmers with a history of crop failures used less fertiliser than farmers who had experienced less destruction', and he concludes that 'only small amounts of fertiliser will be, or for that matter should be, used on paddy rice in Northeast Thailand until the effectiveness of fertiliser is drastically improved by use of high-yielding, fertiliser-responsive, rice varieties in conjunction with proper water control'.

Whatever may be the devices employed for the adoption of productivity enhancing technologies, however, the use of fertiliser and insecticides is an inevitable pre-requisite for entry into the 'sixth hand of farming'.

Both rural and urban elasticities of demand for rice are low and stable in Japan, and in forecasting the need for output reduction Japanese farmers are actively engaged on the conversion of rice culture to horticulture or the production of fodder. Nakamura (undated) writes on the economic effects of using herbicides: 'Around 1949, when herbicides were not yet popularised, 57 per cent of the 2,160 hours taken up for cultivating one hectare of paddy fields were used for weeding, transplanting, and reaping.' Later, with the introduction of herbicides, weeding time was reduced 'from 506 hours, which consisted of removing weeds twice manually and twice by man-power rotary weeder with teeth or tines, to a mere 164 hours, saving the farmer about 110 dollars in terms of money. Therefore, about 80 per cent of all farming families are using herbicides for rice.' But it was in the early 1960s that the first step towards the mixing of several chemicals was taken – fertilisers or insecticides with herbicides – which, in Nakamura's words, 'drove out the weeding by hand and manpower weeder'. He makes the important observation, however, that 'on the other hand, herbicides for upland fields and orchards are considerably behind compared with those for paddy fields'.

Chemical Week records that 'Japan's pesticide output has levelled off reflecting weakness in the home market [indicating that the market is saturated] . . . . Japan's herbicide output, however, rose 23·5 per cent in 1970 and is expected to continue increasing rapidly, spurred by a shortage of agricultural labour' (Anon, 1972).

Producers who subsist at very low levels of income have a higher rate of uptake of weedicides than fertilisers, because no weeds means less labour and more produce, whereas the use of fertilisers means more labour but only more produce given optimum conditions for fertiliser response; and we may make the general observation that the advantages of farming compared to 'city' employment is probably more directly related to the economic bases for protection against crop and livestock diseases (including storage pests), than by any other factor except water.

Ordish and Dufour (1969) suggest that the alternatives open to the farmer threatened with attacks of disease in a crop are five in number.

1. do nothing and harvest what the disease leaves;
2. substitute another crop;
3. grow resistant or immune varieties;
4. protect the crop by spraying, or
5. protect the crop by mechanical methods.

They have further constructed a model to examine the economic effects of blight followed by weevil; this model may be compared with some actual crop losses which occurred in two small areas of Lanao del Sur and Davao del Norte Provinces in Mindanao in 1970.

TABLE 13.7   *Crop losses suffered by a sample of farmers who had not used any protective measures*

Crop	Producers' description of the nature of pest or disease attack	Extent of damage (range) %
Paddy	Stem borer	1–5
	Army worm	3–10
	Rats	0·5–15
Corn (maize)	Stem borer	10–20
	Army worm	8–20
	Rats	5–20

The importance of Ordish's (1952) work is the expression of loss in terms of area loss rather than in money or percentages. It would appear that actual losses in the field of the order of at least 10 to 15 per cent from one cause or another may be expected in virtually all tropical products, wherever the philosophy of 'do nothing and harvest what the disease leaves' prevails – that an unattacked crop is difficult to find outside a plantation economy which normally receives full protection within economic limits and current knowledge.

TABLE 13.8   *Model of crop losses*
(Full crop is one million m.tons, worth on average $100 million grown on 1 million hectares. It is attacked first by blight then by weevil and gives on average 850,000 tons worth $85 million, which just about satisfies the market.)

Pest	% Loss	Loss		Remainder		Land lost		Tons left '000
		Tons '000	Value $'000	Tons '000	Value $'000	From individual pest '000 ha	From both pests	
Blight followed	5	50				50	—	950
by weevil	2·2	21				21	71	929
	5·5	52				52	102	989
	11·1	105				105	155	854
Blight followed	10	100	10,000	900	90,000	100	—	900
by weevil	2·2	20				20	120	880
	5·5	50	5,000	850	85,000	50	150	850
	11·1	100				100	200	800
			15,000 Average					
Blight followed	15	150				150	—	850
by weevil	2·2	19				19	169	831
	5·5	47				47	197	803
	11·1	94				94	244	756

SOURCE: George Ordish and David Dufour, 'Economic bases for protection against plant diseases', *Annual Review of Phytopathology*, 7, (1969) p. 41.

Ordish and Dufour emphasise that

The philosopher must recognise that the real loss is the area of land used but not really needed. For instance, if x acres are used on the average to produce a country's crop of potatoes, and diseases cause a loss of 15 per cent, then, when the disease is conquered, the area could be $x - 15x/100 = 0.85x$ to get the same crop; consequently, the loss in this case is $0.15x$ acres of land and all the seed and effort put into growing the crop.

This loss of effort symbolises for all small farmers in the tropics the whole weakness of their position in relation to even the very minimal of services – a weakness described by Weitz as being 'expressed in a lack of capital, a lack of knowledge, and a lack of initiative'.

CHAPTER 14

Research and Training

The pattern of transformations which the individual farm must undergo is linked to the structure of the national economy; and for every stage in the development of the national economy, there is a corresponding stage in the structure of the individual farm
Ranaan Weitz (1971)

Lack of data from which precise measurements can be made is one of the main short-comings in getting the development process under way. Behrman (1968) attempts some clarifying distinctions in discussing the debate over the supply responsiveness of underdeveloped agriculture, and finds 'no really satisfactory estimates of the marketed surplus response of specific crops, or of total production and marketed surplus responses of total production, because of the data problems which are involved'. Ordish and Dufour (1969) advocate surveys to discover the actual losses which occur because of pests and the actual benefits which accrue as a result of measures taken to control them 'because so little is known of the economics of pest control, particularly in the developing areas from where most of the world's additional food must come'; but even in England it has been found nearly impossible to get a true figure for crop losses from only a single pest. Rhind recalls extensive research at Rothamsted on measuring loss from frit fly on wheat, resulting in no reliable answer. Even with total loss of treated crop the loss cannot be precisely stated, because it is not known what the crop would have yielded without the pest. One can say the loss was 100 per cent, but 100 per cent of what? Only if there is an untreated control is it possible to say with some certainty what has been the treatment benefit.

Further, the profit from the input must be estimated against its cost, and, before making a recommendation, tried out in farmers' hands on their own land. Rhind (1969) particularly emphasises that once farmers have passed the subsistence level of farming

any *production* above their basic necessities is viewed on a strictly profitability level. Consequently, no innovation offered to farmers has any chance of acceptance unless it yields them a profit in one form or another and does not impose too heavy an extra work load. 'The higher the rate of return the higher the rate of adoption.'

A second essential in all extension work is absolute certainty that, except for natural disasters, the new method will *succeed* in farmers' hands. Memories of failures and all they entail to low income groups are long and hard to overcome subsequently. This means it is imperative to test each improvement thoroughly under village conditions.

The problem of translating the results of biological experiments into terms of economic significance has been stressed by De Datta and Barker (1967). For example, a recommendation may call for a complete fertiliser application or a heavy application of certain fertiliser elements or insecticides. The person formulating the recommendation may regard this complete fertilisation or heavy application as an 'insurance' against low yields. From the point of view of the farmer, this same additional input may represent an added cost that seldom pays off or that pays off with relatively low returns and is hence a 'risky investment'. We are also reminded by Dalrymple (1971) in a survey of multiple cropping in less developed nations that although farm chemicals can restore soil fertility and can go a long way towards controlling insects, diseases, and weeds, 'they do so at a direct financial cost to the operator and at longer-run ecological costs'.

But Hopper (1969) points out that the tropical agriculturist has always had a greater array of production options than has the agriculturist located in temperate zones.

> The macro-climatic features that set broad patterns of optimal crop belts in the temperate regions are less rigid in the tropics. . . . Cereal research upset the traditional balance of advantages among tropical crops; the balance will be restored only by a broad frontal attack on the factors limiting yield in the entire array of production alternatives [pulses, oilseeds, fruit and vegetables, root crops, and forages for livestock]. . . .
>
> The economic shelter of the tropical cultivator is the generosity of his environment. If the technology, the water control, the inputs, the credit, available to him permit, he can and will diversify and intensify his farming by selecting from among the rich multitude of tropical crops and livestock alternatives, those he deems most profitable for his twelve-month rotational sequence. . . . The task of public policy for agriculture is to assure that the components of growth and the structure of rural services are functionally capable of supporting a rising output founded on the exploitation of intensive and diversified farming.

In practice, however, benefits invariably differ according to whose point of view is being expressed; high returns from the national view point may appear as low returns to individual farmers on whom the risk-bearing factor may have fallen most heavily; and at its most critical level, we cannot escape the overriding influence of the underemployment effect of low income. The argument that surplus labour exists in much of tropical agriculture which can be withdrawn without loss of output is largely invalidated by the evidence, scarce as it is at present because of the data problems involved, that the marginal productivity of farm family labour is not zero; but the low-income economy which it supports underemploys its human resources, because the dominant sector in almost all countries of the tropics is the family farm business the main characteristic of which is that it is starved of investment finance. This results in low income which in consequence limits the ability of agriculture to finance itself out of profits.

'The attitude that farming is a way of life, rather than a business, stubbornly persists, despite every commercial indication that it is not', states Hicks (1971). 'The significance of this situation is a costly one to the farming industry.' To this dimension must be added the great difficulty of obtaining credit with which almost all farmers in tropical countries are faced wherever they have no rights in land.

'The struggle for land reform in the simple, primary meaning of the term becomes identical with the struggle for change and development', states Weitz, but, he goes on, 'the question is whether this "wonder drug" called "land reform" can actually result in the achievement of the goal of agricultural growth and the development of the rural areas.'

Land reform *per se* has not been found capable of generating an increase in agricultural production. On the contrary, the hidden factor appears to be failure to grasp the reasons for the cultivator's evident preoccupation with any innovation which enables him to shed some of his work load. Whereas the technologist calls for diversification and intensification of agricultural production, the cultivator knows exactly when to stop applying labour under his traditional system of low labour-consuming low productivity farming; and he is not willing to exchange the time-honoured methods for new productivity raising methods which demand greater human effort.

This resistance has its roots in the health status of rural communities who are by and large isolated from the services apparatus, of which chronic shortage of clean water has perhaps the most devastating effects. Much research is needed into the physical energy and economic time devoted to obtaining water. Man's requirement under tropical conditions is more than double that of people living in temperate climates. In many areas, this means head-loading, or at best cycling, from 5 to 10 km – sometimes up to 15 km – which will involve the carrier in a caloric loss, a water loss and a salt loss, all for the sake of one 10 litre bucket on the head, two 10 litre buckets across the shoulder, or four 4 litre cans on a bicycle.

37. A dusty dry-season road causes health hazards to the human population and affects vegetation.

In the process of carrying water, even if it was clean when drawn, it may become contaminated during travel, especially when roads are dusty, or later in households which lack a hygienic system of refuse disposal; and all too often water supply is far from adequate for the whole range of domestic needs.

The effects of waterborne diseases, and of inadequate intake of drinking water and of supplies for personal cleanliness, on the innovatory capacity of the rural work force and on the health of children before entry into the work force is an area of research in urgent need of strengthening, and places high priority on social medicine as an essential element in the services apparatus. Sickness and poverty are common bedfellows, but curative medicine can only be supplied at high cost in terms of doctors, equipment, and hospitals. Weitz (1971) quotes sources for Thailand (Anon, 1963), Malaysia (UN, 1965), and India (Nanavati and Anjaria, 1965):

> In Thailand, for example, there is one doctor for every 800 inhabitants in the capital city of Bangkok, and the ratio for the rural areas is one doctor to 23,000 inhabitants; only 9 of the 1,200 doctors in Malaysia

work in rural areas; and in India three-quarters of the doctors are concentrated in the urban areas, which contain only a quarter of the population. . . . To raise the standard of services in the rural areas, qualified
manpower is needed to operate them, but such people are unwilling to
live in the villages precisely because of the low level of services found
there.

In seeking a new approach in this much neglected field of physical
planning research in rural areas, a necessary element in rural training
programmes should be a practical course in social medicine, with
selected villages as pilot areas for the collection of basic data. In a
thorough socio-economic survey in 1969 of 244 households in
Agusan, Mindanao, (Anon, 1971) data was collected on sources of
drinking water which showed that 68·8 per cent of the households get
their drinking water from open wells, 12·3 per cent from springs, 10
per cent from rain, and 4·1 per cent from rivers and creeks. 'These
sources of drinking water,' the investigators report, 'are subject to
contamination and/or are easily liable as sources of harmful germs.'

38. A motor vehicle while taking grain and Coca-Cola to drought-stricken
villages in Northeast Thailand gets bedded down in the dry sandy soil, because
there are no feeder roads on which to travel.

39. The headman of a northeast Thai **village** quenches the thirst of the children with one sip each of water – a **strictly** rationed commodity in the long dry season.

40. At the height of the dry season: boy carting water back to his village for drinking and other domestic purposes – collected earlier from a polluted pond in which he had also taken a bath.

Only 4·1 per cent had 'safe' drinking water from pump wells. The survey further revealed that more than half the respondent households do not have latrines, and that toilet generally is not yet recognised as a need of every home.

Details of members of the survey households who had died as of March 1970, were also recorded – 62 per cent of the households having had one death each; 16 per cent two deaths each; 11 per cent three deaths each; and the remainder four or more deaths per household. Of reported deaths more than a third died in infancy, and a further third between the age of 1 and 4 years; a further 12 per cent died within the age group 5 to 9 years. Thus the survey population were found to be relatively young, the mean age of members of the survey households being only 30 years; in consequence, 'the burden of dependency for the economically active members of the survey population is heavy'. Causes of death were various, the most common of which were high fever, dysentery, el tor cholera, bronchopneumonia, and malaria.

To the climatic hazard in tropical rural areas, therefore, must be added the health hazard. Amelioration of these two factors, which together constitute one of the main constraints to agricultural development, will come more rapidly and more readily through involvement of rural trainees at the 'grass roots' level than by any amount of theoretical training in remote institutions.

In point of fact, in all aspects of modernisation and development of the rural sector, the first criterion must be one of data collection; and because it is time-consuming and demands that the results are reliable in that the ability of an economy to modernise is directly proportional to the quality of the basic information that is fed into the development plan, the incorporation of this activity into the curricula of rural training institutions would facilitate continuous recording by successive intakes of students working under close supervision.

On taking up his appointment as Professor of Indian Economics in the University of Madras in December 1915, Gilbert Slater (1918) determined to direct the attention of students towards the study of particular villages. In February 1916 he had his first opportunity of seeing something of Indian village life, when he accompanied one of his senior students on a visit to the student's village. On the basis of his observations in this village, Slater drew up a 'village questionnaire', had notebooks made up with the questions typed, interleaved with blank pages, and dealt them out to students who undertook to make surveys of their native villages during the long vacation. He had found on reaching Madras that students looked on economics as a 'fairly easy option for degree getting, and as consisting of a series of unintelligible theories to be learnt parrot fashion from Marshall's *Principles*, with no relation to actual life in India if anywhere else'. Slater wanted to make his students regard economics as 'concerned with ordinary contemporary Indian life, with as its central object of study the causes of, and remedies for, Indian poverty'. To incite them to survey their native villages seemed to him a simple way of achieving this result.

It has been too readily assumed in many aid programmes and government development plans that such institutions as agricultural education, extension services, and credit, would induce change in the rate of absorption of new agricultural factors. Luning (1969) cites the instance of the 'technically-oriented extension officer' who can make a fundamental error in his technical approach in an area where land is relatively abundant if he stresses maximum return to land and objects to the farmers' low yield per hectare. 'In fact, the farmer may act quite rationally in optimizing the scarcest resource – labour.'

Extension has come to mean the ability to put across to the farmer the findings of research and the new input forms which will achieve higher output per unit of area; but for the farmer it has often appeared as an alien authority telling him what to do, when what is needed is some catalyst device which will generate growth from within the farming sector itself.

Much of the emphasis on training has been on imparting a knowledge of improved cultural practices in respect of indigenous crops, and the techniques of production of suitable new crops; but for the young, the majority of whom are destined to be reinstated on the family farm with little responsibility and no authority, this type of training does not appeal. Different courses are needed which will turn out a virtual army of semiskilled personnel equipped to forge vital links in the chain between the growing demands of urbanisation and the farmer in his all too often grossly underserviced and even unserviced rural habitat.

The problem may be illustrated in part from the firsthand observations of the rice-milling industry which were made by Uma Lele (1971). She found that because of high variable costs milling is predominantly a trading operation which involves mainly storage, and that only a small value is added in actual processing.

What is disturbing is the central role played by traders in village and primary wholsesale markets who operate as 'holding agents' and 'price fixers', because of their unique position as a business elite and as a class elite (they invariably also own land). This state of affairs provides only the flimsiest edifice in the structure which links the individual farmer with the national economy; the proliferation of middle men which trading under conditions of poor road networks and poorly equipped local markets generates is not conducive to the achievement of a healthy rural–urban structure.

Yet Bauer (1971) points out that

> in emerging economies, distribution – especially small-scale trade – is more labour-intensive than many or even most other activities outside the subsistence sector. This is so partly because unskilled labour can be substituted more readily for capital in small-scale distribution than elsewhere. . . . There is no reason for disparaging labour-intensive activities in these societies. But at the same time there is no general case either for encouraging or subsidising an activity simply because it is

labour-intensive. There is no merit in encouraging such an activity unless there is a market for the output at a price higher than its real cost in terms of the alternative uses of the resources employed in its production.

If entrepreneurship is the missing component – for example in the establishment of processing enterprises and inputs services – we might agree with Heseltine (1971) who states for Madagascar that the obstacles to development, apart from the transport difficulties, lie in the capacity to mobilise resources and productivity in the modern sense of 'mangement'. 'The potential for such a mobilisation is certainly to be found in the human capital represented by the Malagasy population,' he goes on to say; 'in its capacity for education and in the dynamism it has always shown towards accepting and utilising knowledge introduced from outside.'

The Madagascar agricultural economy sets the scene for many tropical countries, potentially or in fact, although as Heseltine points out, there are some important differences in kind.

The chief particularities (of the economy of Madagascar) may be summarised as: stable and generally adequate production of basic foodstuff, rice; diversity of production patterns due to ecological factors; wide range of export products; considerable internal exchanges of food-crops; and appearance of mixed farming in isolated areas.

The country is fortunate in possessing a

favourable hydrology over most of the island with a reliable rainfall. ... The unfavourable factors are that these communities are widely scattered and are linked by indifferent communications, which poses problems of marketing. Traditional marketing structures still result in the peasant's receiving low prices for his products and paying high prices for what he buys. Incentives are thus limited by market opportunities.

Madagascar also has a high cattle population. Heseltine states that 'since 1940, the national herd has slowly increased, aided by considerable improvements in animal disease control introduced by the veterinary service'. Distances from factory and market presents problems, however, and animals from the west coast have to travel very long distances on foot and suffer heavy weight losses. Meat consumption is relatively high, and Heseltine quotes Lacroutz who has estimated that 75,000 head of cattle from the producing western region travel each year for consumption on the east coast. Heseltine refers to Lacroutz's figures of total consumption of meat and offal per head per annum (1962): rural population 22·1 kg, small towns 28·0 kg, and large towns 37·3 kg. The large cattle population began to be utilised in 1889, Heseltine records, 'when the first meat factory was established at Antongombato near Diego–Suarez. ... The elements are there, with the large supplies of cattle and pigs, and some experience in running factory and canning operations, and it is certain that present plans being carried out by the Government will rapidly expand production in this sector.' The economic rationale for live-stock producers in tropical areas will be to 'export' from producing areas on the hook rather than the hoof.

In Madagascar, the most modern and best-equipped agro-industry, however, is the sugar industry, but this is

> essentially a plantation operation, export-orientated, in which small planters participate much less than on Mauritius, where about 15 per cent of the factory capacity is supplied by small planters. In Madagascar, the bulk of the cane used is grown by the companies on their own land with highly developed irrigation systems . . . . The capacity for sugar produc-tion is much greater but is limited by world markets. Internal consumption is limited by the price (approximately $US 0·25 per kilo), which makes Madagascar the tenth most expensive country in the world for sugar (Anon, *Plan Quinquennial 1964–69*).

It is evident that the price is fixed to subsidise in part the cost of production and profit levels of the companies, which have monopoly powers conferred on them by the government under this arrangement.

'Other processing industries include oil expressing plants, and treating coconut and cotton seed for local consumption. . . . Since independence in 1960, and with considerable Government support, a number of new small industries have been set up to supply the local market.' Additionally, Madagascar has a considerable tourist potential in concert with many other island economies.

Nevertheless, Heseltine finds the problems to be similar to those in other developing and predominantly agricultural countries:

> . . . reluctance of nationals to invest their savings other than in real estate; small inelastic local markets; high cost of transport and of certain essential raw materials. This is aggravated by the very high cost of energy. . . . The high cost of electrical energy is due in part to the limited demand; in turn, the cost itself limits the demand.

The findings of research in Thailand indicate that there is a close correlation between the percentage of cultivated area which is irrigated and the widespread usage of industrial inputs; but a report on a farm management survey conducted under the auspices of the Royal Irrigation Department (NEDECO, 1969) records that although their adoption occurred rapidly over a decade this was from quite limited bases near Bangkok. Furthermore, the report continues, 'although the introduction of irrigation has stimulated the cultivation of transplanted rice, the irrigation facilities are far from adequate to obtain satisfactory yields. The unreliable water supply early in the season and the improper water control later onwards are serious constraints.'

We have here two factors: firstly, the pull effect of a highly urbanised capital city in the creation of a demand for technically skilled manpower with administrative ability, with command over financial resources and the willingness to invest in farm-factory-consumer linked industries. Data are dismally lacking on the spatial structure of the economic services apparatus available at local levels – the rate of growth of small towns and their potential as magnets for public and private sector investment in infrastructural development, and agribusiness.

The 'sixth hand of farming', in which farmers follow modernised practices, including the use of mechanical equipment and hired labour, and produce entirely for the market, renders the farmer, however good an entrepreneur he may be, virtually dependent on the supporting economic services apparatus for the success of his farm business. A society in which the majority of its farmers have reached this stage has made the irrevocable break with the low income agricultures associated with the subsistence sectors of tropical countries.

The second factor with which we are concerned is the actual contribution on-farm of public sector activities. Whitehead (1971) quotes Myrdal (1968): 'The state does not want to take the role of enterpriser, but rather to help provide enterprise to take charge of transforming the economy of the country . . . changes in technology have tended to greatly increase the requirements for public utility investments'; but, Whitehead adds, 'even where the state sector extends beyond the field of public utilities it does not normally present a threat to private enterprise'.

The public sector fails conspicuously, however, wherever an unbridgeable gap occurs between the service provided – say an irrigation headwork, a super-highway, a banking facility – and the individual farmer who cannot make use of the service because of unreliable water supply, or impassable feeder roads, or lack of mortgageable assets; these are among the most common constraints experienced by those farmers who are trapped in the economic rut of the third and fourth 'hands' of farming. To this state of affairs must be added the uncertainty factor which is endemic in all peasant farming.

Using a linear programming model and sensitivity analysis, Heyer (1972) analyses the impact of cotton on a traditional food crop system in a semi-arid area of Kenya. She argues that

in general the outcome of any particular set of peasant farm production decisions depends both on these decisions and of unforeseeable variations in inputs and outputs that occur during the production period. Inputs may not be as planned because sickness affects labour inputs, unavailability of purchased inputs at the required time delays or makes fruitless their applications, pests and diseases disrupt input patterns, and so on. Outputs are affected by deviations from planned input patterns. They are also affected by climate, pests, diseases, and market conditions even if all inputs are applied as planned.

Such an analysis as that made by Heyer requires a complete set of data. This she collected through the year September 1962–63. Sixteen holdings were chosen to represent important production activities and different standards of management; and the data for analysis were collected in twice weekly visits to the farms. The value of this exercise lies in the important policy implications that emerge from the analysis, which reinforces the argument for introducing data collecting as an integral part of all rural training programmes (in addition to and not in place of specialist courses designed to meet a demand for particular skills) – an inescapable byproduct of which is the involvement of the student in his environment. To enable him to analyse and interpret data, he will also require to learn at least the less sophisticated tools of analysis and how to apply them in practice.

Programmes which are oriented towards the establishment of advisory services, which link the results of those engaged in research with those engaged in field work, have a greater opportunity of making a significant impact on development of the rural sector than has the establishment of an extension service which appears as an arm of a centralised authority; Dimaano and Guzman (1967) pinpoint the cleavage between the farmer and the extension worker when they say that 'very often extension workers make the mistake of introducing something to the barrio [village] people just because it is new even if it does not fit the needs of the farmers'. The most frequent reason for non-adoption of a recommended farm practice they found was the incompatibility or non-applicability of the practice to existing conditions. Practical demonstration on farmers' own land appears to be the only extension method likely to succeed until the complete confidence of farmers has been gained. For farmers who are operating close to the poverty line lack reserves to cushion a failure resulting from use of an unfamiliar practice; and the risk is too great as its effects are felt by all members of the family. When he is confident that 'something new will work in his hands and will pay', the farmer is seldom slow to respond.

The initiation of wideranging surveys of existing conditions in rural sectors may be expected to lead to hitherto unrevealed sources of managerial and innovatory capacity. This is likely to be especially so among those younger members of the economically active age group who, in the absence of employment openings elsewhere to which they can migrate, are consciously or subconsciously searching for stimuli at local levels which will generate growth from within the given range of production possibilities.

Definitions

Average product per man-hour: total product divided by the total number of hours of labour applied to the same land.

Marginal product per man-hour: the additional product obtained when an additional man-hour of labour is applied to the same land.

Disguised unemployment: the state of affairs which exists when the same output could be produced using *less* labour. In this case the marginal product of labour is zero. A less extreme form of disguised unemployment is found when labour continues to work on family farms (or, sometimes, in certain other types of business) at a marginal productivity which, while not zero, is well below wages currently payable for such work.

Income elasticity of demand: the proportional change in the quantity of a good bought divided by the proportional change in income, price remaining the same.

Price elasticity of demand: the proportional change in the quantity of a good bought divided by the proportional change in the price of the good, money income remaining the same. If the proportional change in quantity is less than the proportional change in price, demand is said to be inelastic; if the proportional change in quantity is greater than the proportional change in price, demand is said to be elastic. Price elesticity depends upon the possibilities of substitution. It is generally greater when substitution is easy. In low-income groups, however, there are few substitution possibilities.

Real income: the goods and services which a person can buy with his money income. With a *given* money income, real income will be higher when prices are low and vice versa.

Paddy equivalent: this is the natural unit for measuring real product in tropical communities in which the greater part of the output is grain, grown for subsistence consumption with only a small and unrepresentative part of it traded for money. Since the output of other products is comparatively small and uncertainties about their valuation unlikely to affect the result appreciably, these are converted into grain equivalents at the rate at which they exchange against grain in local markets.

Conversion Factors

1 kilometre	= 0·621372 miles
1 mile	= 1·609 kilometres
1 hectare	= 2·4711 acres
1 acre	= 0·4047 hectares
100 hectares	= 1 square kilometre
640 acres	= 1 square mile
1 square kilometre	= 0·3861 square miles
1 square mile	= 2·590 square kilometres
1 kilogramme	= 2·2046 lb
1 lb	= 0·4536 kilogrammes
1 metric ton	= 1,000 kilogrammes
1 long ton	= 2,240 lb
1 short ton	= 2,000 lb
1 long ton	= 1·016 metric tons
1 short ton	= 0·9072 metric tons
1 metric ton	= 0·9842 long tons
1 metric ton	= 1·1023 short tons
1 metric ton kilometre	= 0·6116 long ton miles
1 metric ton kilometre	= 0·6849 short ton miles
1 long ton mile	= 1·635 metric ton kilometres
1 short ton mile	= 1·460 metric ton kilometres
1 millimetre	= 0·03937 inches
1 inch	= 25·40 millimetres
1 centimetre	= 0·39370 inches
1 inch	= 2·540 centimetres
1 cubic centimetre	= 0·06102 cubic inches
1 cubic inch	= 16·387 cubic centimetres
1 cubic metre	= 35·314 cubic feet
1 cubic foot	= 0·02832 cubic metres
1 litre	= 1·7607 pints
1 pint	= 0·56795 litres
1 litre	= 0·2201 gallons
1 gallon	= 4·5436 litres

To convert: into:
°Fahrenheit   °Centigrade: subtract 32, multiply by 5, and divide by 9.
°Centigrade   °Fahrenheit: multiply by 9, divide by 5, and add 32.

Bibliography

ANON. (1963) *Public Health in Thailand*, Thailand Ministry of Public Health.
—— (1968) 'Rice marketing in the Philippines: crop year 1967–68', *Rice and Corn Administration*.
—— (1968) *The Greater Manila Terminal Food Market, A Feasibility Study*, Development Bank of the Philippines.
—— (1970) *Plan Quinquennial, 1964–1969*, and *Programmes des Grandes Operations*, Commissariat-General au Plan.
—— (1970) *Manpower Planning Division of the Economic Development Board*, Bangkok.
—— (1971) *Total Population of the Philippines and Each Province, City, Municipality and Municipal District – 1970*, Bureau of the Census and Statistics, Republic of the Philippines.
—— (1971) *A Socio-Economic Survey of 244 Households in the Agusan Resettlement Area in 1969*, Committee on the Mindanao Agricultural Resettlement Agency Project, Community Development Research Council, University of the Philippines, mimeo.
—— (1972) 'Greener pastures for pesticides overseas?' *Markets, Chemical Week*, 15 March, 27–8.
ARB, Y. (1971) 'Types of agricultural projects used in developing countries', in R. Weitz, ed., *Rural Development in a Changing World*, Massachusetts Institute of Technology Press.
BANKS, A. L. (1969) 'Catastrophes and restraints', in J. Hutchinson, ed., *Population and Food Supply: essays on human needs and agricultural prospects*, Cambridge University Press.
BAUER, P. T. (1971) *Dissent on Development: studies and debates in development economics*, Weidenfeld & Nicolson.
BAUER, P. T. and YAMEY, B. S. (1961) 'Economic progress and occupational distribution', *Economic J.*, 741–755.
BEHRMAN, J. R. (1968) *Supply Response in Underdeveloped Agriculture: a case study of four major annual crops in Thailand, 1937–1963*, North-Holland Publishing Company.
BOSERUP, E. (1965) *The Conditions of Agricultural Growth: the economics of agrarian change under population pressure*, Allen & Unwin.
BROWN, D. D. (1971) *Agricultural Development in India's Districts*, Harvard University Press; London, Oxford University Press.
BUCHANAN, R. M. and PUGH, J. C. (1955) *Land and People in Nigeria: the human geography of Nigeria and its environmental background*, University of London Press.
CABRENA, R. M. (undated) 'Farm Management, Land Use and Tenancy in Simaya, Nabago and Macote, Bukidnon, Mindanao (Philippines), 1960', unpublished thesis, Mindanao Agricultural College.
CARRUTHERS, I. D. (1968) 'Irrigation development planning: aspects of Pakistan experience', Wye College, University of London: *Agrarian Development Studies Report No. 2*.
CERNOHOUS, Z. (1966) 'The marketing of agricultural products in the Philippines', *Philippine Economic Journal*, 5(1), 64–94.
CLARK, COLIN (1967) *Population Growth and Land Use*, Macmillan,
—— and HASWELL, MARGARET (1970) *The Economics of Subsistence Agriculture*, Macmillan, 4th edn.

CLAYTON, E. (1963) *Economic Planning in Peasant Agriculture*, Wye College, University of London.

CONKLIN, H. C. (1957) 'Hanunoo agriculture: a report on an integral system of shifting cultivation in the Philippines', *FAO Forestry Development Paper No. 12*.

CURTIN, T. R. C. (1969) 'The economics of population growth and control in developing countries', *Rev. Soc. Economy*, **27** (2), 139–53.

DALRYMPLE, D. G. (1971) 'Survey of multiple-cropping in less-developed Nations', U.S. Dept. Agric. co-operating with U.S. Agency for *Int. Dev. FEDR–12*.

DE DATTA, S. K. and BARKER, R. (1967) *Management Practices and Economic Analysis of Experimental Results in Rice Production*, International Rice Research Institute Conference.

DIMAANO, C. M. and GUZMAN, A. M. (1967) *Coralan Rice Farmers' Response to Change in Cropping Pattern: A Case Study*, International Rice Research Institute Conference, December 8–9.

DIMACUTAC, B. and ESCALANTE, C. (undated) 'Farm prices of selected farm products at Sinanguyan, Kitaotao and Dangcagan, Bukidnon, Mindanao (Philippines), 1963–64,' unpublished paper, Mindanao Agricultural College.

DOMIKE, A. L. and TOKMAN, V. E. (1971) 'The role of agricultural taxation in financing agricultural development in Latin America', in K. Griffin, ed., *Financing Development in Latin America*, Macmillan.

DOVRING, F. (1969) *Land Reform and Productivity: The Mexican Case*, University of Illinois Department of Agricultural Economics, AERR 83, Nov. 1966, mimeo; revised version as Univ. of Wisconsin Land Tenure Center, LTC 61, Jan. 1969, mimeo.

——— (1970) 'Land reform in Mexico', *Agency for International Development: Spring Review*, SR/LR/C–1, mimeo.

DUCKHAM, A. N. and MASEFIELD, G. B. (1970) *Farming Systems of the World*, Chatto & Windus.

FAO (1966) *Agricultural Development in Modern Japan*, Rome: Agricultural Planning Studies No. 6.

FLETCHER, L. B., GRABER, E., MERRILL, W. C. and THORBECKE, E. (1970) *Guatemala's Economic Development: the role of agriculture*, Iowa State University Press.

FREEMAN, J. D. (1955) 'Iban agriculture', HMSO, *Colonial Office Research Studies, No. 18*.

FUCHS, F. W. and VINGERHOETS, J. (1971) *Report of the Working Group on Rural Manpower and Employment*, prepared by Manpower Planning Division of the National Economic Development Board, Rural Sector, mimeo.

GOYOAGA, J. (1971) 'Social differentiation in Ayutthaya Town', *Chulalongkorn University Social Science Research Institute, J. Soc. Sci.*, Special Issue (July), 317–327.

HARDOY, J. E. (1967) 'Argentina', in *Urban Agglomerations in the States of the Third World: their political, social and economic role*, Collection de l'Institut International des Civilisations Differentes, Report of the 34th Incidi Study Session.

HASWELL, M. R. (1953) 'Economics of Agriculture in a Savannah Village', HMSO, *Colonial Research Studies, No. 8*.

——— (1963) 'The changing pattern of economic activity in a Gambia village', HMSO, *Department of Technical Co-operation Overseas Research Publication No. 2*.

——— (1967) *Economics of Development in Village India*, Routledge & Kegan Paul.

——— (1970) *Potential for Economic Growth of Resource Development in Asian Agriculture*, SEATO, Bangkok.

164   *Tropical Farming Economics*

———— (1972) 'Transport of vegetable crops in developing countries: the need for better roads', *Span*, 15 (2), 79–80.
———— (1973) 'Adverse Effect of Sickness on Tropical Agriculture', in *Resources and Population*, The Eugenics Society, London.
HAYAMI, Y. and RUTTAN, V. W. (1971) *Agricultural Development: An International Perspective*, Johns Hopkins Press.
HESELTINE, N. (1965) 'Investment in agriculture', *World Crops*, 17 (4), 24–31.
———— (1971) *Madagascar*, Pall Mall Press.
HEYER, J. (1972) 'An analysis of peasant farm production under conditions of uncertainty', *J. Agric. Econ.*, 23 (2), 135–46.
HICKS, N. (1971) 'Outside Investment in Agriculture: Sources in the Developed Countries', *Span*, 14 (3), 150–52.
HODDER, B. W. (1968) *Economic Development in the Tropics*, Methuen.
HOFFMAN, H. F. J. (1967) *Case Studies of Progressive Farming in Central Malawi*, Government of Malawi.
HOLMBERG, A. R. (1950) 'Nomads of the long bow: the Siriono of eastern Bolivia', *Smithsonian Institution of Social Anthropology Publication No. 10*.
HOPPER, W. D. (1969) *The Promise of Abundance*, Regional Seminar on Agriculture, Asian Development Bank, Sydney, April 10–12.
HUTCHINSON, J. (1969) *Population and Food Supply: Essays on Human Needs and Agricultural Prospects*, Cambridge University Press.
ILO (1970) *Towards Full Employment*, A Programme for Colombia, prepared by an Inter-Agency Team.
ISHIKAWA, S. (1967) *Economic Development in Asian Perspective*, Tokyo, Hitotsubashi University.
JACKSON, C. A. (1971) *The Tomato Canning Industry in Nigeria*, Paper presented at the Vegetable Crops Seminar co-sponsored by The International Institute for Tropical Agriculture, L'Institut de Recherches Agronomiques Tropicales et des Cultures Vivrieres, and the Ford Foundation, Ibadan.
JACOBY, E. H. (1971) *Man and Land: the fundamental issue in development*, Deutsch.
JOHNSTON, B. F. (1966) 'Agriculture and economic development: the relevance of the Japanese experience', *Food Research Institute Studies*, VI (3).
———— (1971) 'Criteria for the design of agricultural development strategies', Paper presented at the Japan Economic Research Center Conference on Agriculture and Economic Development, Tokyo and Hakone, 6–10 September.
KOLSHUS, H. J. (1972), 'Modernisation of paddy rice farming in Northeast Thailand with special reference to use of fertilizer', unpublished thesis, Graduate School, University of Kentucky.
LACROUTZ, M. *et al.* (1962) *L'Elevage et la commercialisation du betail et de la viande à Madagascar*, Paris; Ministère de la Cooperation.
LELE, U. (1971) *Food Grain Marketing in India: private performance and public policy*, Cornell University Press.
LUNING, H. A. (1969) *The Economic Transformation of Family Rice-Farming in Surinam (South America)*, Dept. Agric. Econ. of the Tropics and Sub-tropics, Agricultural University, Wageningen.
MARTIN, ANNE (1963) 'The marketing of minor crops in Uganda', HMSO, *Department of Technical Co-operation Overseas Research Publication No. 1*.
MYRDAL, G. (1968) *Asian Drama: an inquiry into the poverty of nations*, Allen Lane, The Penguin Press.
NAKAMURA, H. (undated) 'The Movement of Herbicides in Japan', Nihon-Nohyaku Co. Ltd., 1–10.
NANAVATI, M. B. and ANJARIA, J. J. (1965) *The Indian Rural Problem*, 6th revised edn, Bombay, Indian Society of Agricultural Economics.

NEDECO (1969) 'Report on the Farm Management Survey', *Kingdom of Thailand, Royal Irrigation Department, Land Consolidation Project: The Chao Phya Farm Management Survey, Phase II*, 1–61.

NORMAN, D. W. (1967) 'Land and labour in three Zaria villages', *Samaru Agricultural Newsletter*, **9** (3), 28–35.

―――― (1968) 'How hard do Nigerian farmers work?' *Samaru Agricultural Newsletter*, **10** (2), 18–28.

―――― (1970) 'Labour inputs of farmers: A case study of the Zaria province of the North-Central State of Nigeria', *Samaru Research Bulletin*, **116**, 3–14.

ORDISH, G. (1952) *Untaken Harvest*, Constable.

―――― and DUFOUR, D. (1969) 'Economic bases for protection against plant diseases', *Annual Review of Phytopathology*, **7**, 31–50.

PEDLER, F. J. (1955) *Economic Geograpy of West Africa*, Longmans.

PELZER, K. J. (1954) *Pioneer Settlements in the Asiatic Tropics*, New York.

PETERS, D. U. (1950) 'Land usage in Serenge district', *Rhodes–Livingstone Paper No. 19*.

PHILIPPS, P. G. (1954) 'The metabolic cost of common West African agricultural activities', *J. Trop. Med. and Hyg.*, **57** (12), 12–20.

PLATT, B. S. (1946) *Nyasaland Nutrition Survey: 1938–39*, Colonial Office Library, mimeo.

RHIND, D. (1969) 'Report on the SEATO Regional Agricultural Research Project', SEATO, Bangkok, **1**, 1–106.

ROSAURO, P. J. (1961) 'Elasticities of consumption and the concentration of expenditures in rural Philippines', *Statistical Reporter* (Manila, National Economic Council) **5**, no. 4, 22–7.

RUFENER, W. H. (1971) 'Cattle and water buffalo production in villages of North-east Thailand', unpublished thesis, University of Illinois.

SACHS, R. and GLEES, A. (1967) 'Preservation of wildlife, utilisation of wild animals and processing of game meat', Government of the Federal Republic of Germany, *Tanzania Project FE 428*, 20 pp.

SANDOVAL, P. R., HSIEH, S. C. and GAON, B. V. (1967) 'Productivity status of lowland rice farms: a case study of pre-land reform conditions', *The Philippine Agriculturist*, **2** (June), 1–19.

SANGHVI, P. (1969) *Surplus Manpower in Agriculture and Economic Development*, London, Asia Publishing House.

SCHULTZ, T. W. (1964) *Transforming Traditional Agriculture*, Yale University Press.

―――― (1971) *Investment in Human Capital: the role of education and of research*, New York, The Free Press; London, Collier-Macmillan.

SCOVILLE, O. J. (1972) 'Farm and agribusiness relationships in economic development', unpublished paper, Department of Agricultural Economics, Kansas State University.

SLATER, G. (1918) *Some South Indian Villages*, University of Madras.

STOKES, C. J. (1968) *Transportation and Economic Development in Latin America*, Praeger.

TAKASE, K. and KANŌ, T. (1969) 'Development strategy of irrigation and drainage', in *Asian Agricultural Survey*, The Asian Development Bank.

TANAKA, K. (1963) 'Two patterns of short-run supply behaviour of the subsistence farm', *Rural Economic Problems*.

THUROW, L. C. (1971) 'Development finance in Latin America: basic principles', in K. Griffin, ed., *Financing Development in Latin America*, Macmillan.

TROWELL, H. C. (1955) 'Calorie and protein requirements of adult male Africans', *E. Afr. Med. J.*, **32** (5), 153–63.

TURNHAM, D. (1970) *The Employment Problem in Less Developed Countries: A Review of Evidence*, OECD.

UNITED NATIONS (1965) *Economic Survey of Asia and the Far East*, ECAFE.

────── (1969) 'Growth of the world's urban and rural population, 1920–2000', New York, *Population Studies No. 44*.

VAN DUSSELDORP, D. B. W. M. (1971) *Planning of Service Centres in Rural Areas of Developing Countries*, Wageningen, International Institute for Land Reclamation and Improvement.

VON OPPENFELD, H. *et al.*, (1957) 'Farm management, land use and tenancy in the Philippines', *Central Experiment Station Bulletin 1*.

WEITZ, R. (1971) *From Peasant to Farmer: a revolutionary strategy for development*, Columbia University Press.

WHITEHEAD, L. (1971) 'Public sector activities', in K. Griffin, ed., *Financing Development in Latin America*, Macmillan.

WRIGLEY, G. (1971) *Tropical Agriculture: The Development of Production*, 3rd edn, Faber.

YOUNGSON, A. J. (1967) *Overhead Capital: a study in development economics*, Edinburgh University Press.

Index